2

PUBLIC HEALTH IN THE 21ST CENTURY

POVERTY ALLEVIATION AND CONVENTIONAL MFIS

CHALLENGES AND PROSPECTS

PUBLIC HEALTH IN THE 21ST CENTURY

Additional books and e-books in this series can be found on Nova's website under the Series tab.

PUBLIC HEALTH IN THE 21ST CENTURY

POVERTY ALLEVIATION AND CONVENTIONAL MFIS

CHALLENGES AND PROSPECTS

MOHAMMAD ALI ASHRAF, PHD

nova science publishers
New York

NOTICE TO THE READER

Additional color graphics may be available in the e-book version of this book.

Library of Congress Cataloging-in-Publication Data

ISBN: 978-1-53615-044-5

Published by Nova Science Publishers, Inc. † New York

To the poor who are struggling for their survival

CONTENTS

LIST OF FIGURES

List of Tables

PREFACE

Poverty has been a buzzword in Bangladesh since the early period of 1970s when the people of the country fought for its independence. After the independence in 1971 the country fell into the grips of a famine in 1974 which shook us all to the core of our being. News media reported horrible stories of death and starvation in remote villages and district towns across the new country, Bangladesh. At this juncture of history, Professor Muhammad Yunus came to the forefront and taught the poor how to fight against poverty with 'microcredit'. Following this fact, the 'Grameen Bank' came into reality in October 2, 1983 with interest-based microcredit program which later conventionally known as 'microfinance' program, distinctly different from Islamic microfinance institutes. Since then the Grameen Model has been replicated by myriads of NGOs and conventional microfinance institutes (MFIs) domestically and globally to eradicate poverty from society. Though it has been about four decades since its inception as a full-fledged Bank, this turns as a legitimate question – how far are these NGO-MFIs successful to attain their core objective of poverty alleviation? Or, are there any hurdles for which they are facing challenges to reach the objectives? And what are the possible solutions or prospects that they may have? This book is primarily an inquiry into seeking the possible answers of those fundamental questions through investigating the participation of the rural poor especially rural poor women in NGO-MFIs in Bangladesh.

This book explicates empirical case studies and ethnographic information on Big-Four powerful development organizations, such as BRAC (Bangladesh Rural Advancement Committee), ASA (Association for Social Advancement), Proshika (Centre for Human Development) and the Grameen Bank in Bangladesh. It examines issues of poverty alleviation through the participation of rural poor women in NGO-MFIs and the hurdles they face to participate in these NGO-MFIs. The perspective of an econometric approach is used in this book for the analysis of the empirical materials. Research findings show that there has been participation problem arising from both sides of the clients and the programs of microfinance which are not effective in alleviating rural poverty (Ashraf, 2011c; Karim, 2011; Huq, 2001; Evans et al. 1999).

This book covers a wide range of socio-economic and religious contexts in order to explore a series of issues relating to the dynamics of participation and nonparticipation, intention, attitudes, social norms, perceived behavioral control of rural poor women located in six districts of Bangladesh. The study areas were selected randomly at two levels. First, six divisions were selected randomly from the total of nine divisions in Bangladesh. Then six districts were selected randomly from six divisions. The districts are Nilphamari, Bogra, Kishoreganj, Maulovibazar, Shariatpur and Satkhira. These six districts were chosen because the people of these regions are poorer and more vulnerable than those in other regions of Bangladesh (Mahmud, 2010). Due to these demographic concerns, the MFIs are operating microfinance programs there (MRA, 2011). These six districts comprised individuals of participating and nonparticipating poor in the villages who were predominantly peasants, rickshaw (3-wheel cart) or van pullers and day laborers.

Recent evidence suggests that Bangladesh has done tremendously well in reducing poverty and microfinance has been trumpeted as a champion over the last three decades for attaining the global objectives of alleviating rural poverty and improving women's socioeconomic status (Ashraf, 2013; Karim, 2011). Until now, there have been large number of empirical and quasi-empirical evidence which supports this view on a positive role of microfinance institutes (MFIs) in poverty alleviation such as Hossain (1984, 1986, 1989, 1998), Khandker (1996, 1998), Pitt and Khandker (1995, 1998), Hashemi, Schuler and Reley (1996), Zohir (2001), Khandker (2003), Razzaque (2010) and many others. However, this trumpeted role of microfinance appears to be dull to this day (Karim, 2011) because of the criticisms which stem from different issues such as economic impact (Morduch, 1998, 1999; Hulme and Mosley, 1996; Haque and Yamao, 2008; Khosa, 2007) and social impact on women's status (Rahman, 1996; Rahman, 1999; Fernando, 2006; Muhammad, 2006). Recently, PKSF conclusively remarked that poverty in Bangladesh has not been reduced by MFIs which have some socioeconomic and religious hindrances (Osmani et al., 2015). This book is simply a single effort to unveil those factors faced by MFIs.

Drawing on the evidence stated above, the present study is empirically investigating the factors that influence nonparticipation and participation of the rural poor in microfinance with intention as a mediator using theory of planned behavior. The conceptual model tested had eight explanatory variables (i.e., challenges that MFIs are facing) in addition to the original components of actual behavior, intention, attitude, subjective norms and PBC. The additional eight variables (challenges) were: (1) fear of risk associated with loans borrowed from microfinance programs, (2) individual preferences in microfinance programs, (3) religious leaders' lecture on Islamic principles, (4) spousal dislike of female heading the household (5) friends' advice, (6) insufficiency of resources, (7) lack of business knowledge, and (8) poor health or vulnerability to crisis. To attain its objectives, the study applied logistic regression technique along with multiple regression analyses.

Results indicated that attitudes and PBC significantly influenced intention of nonparticipation of the rural poor in MFIs, while intention and nonparticipation were negatively related. Subjective norm and perceived behavioral control (PBC) were not statistically significant to influence intention. Among the external variables, it was found that several challenge factors, namely, fear of risks associated with loans, individual preference of taking loan, spousal dislike as female head of household, insufficiency of resources, and lack of knowledge have significant impact on the nonparticipation of the rural poor in MFIs in Bangladesh. Of 13 hypotheses developed, only seven received empirical support while six did not.

LIST OF ABBREVIATIONS

ADB	Asian Development Bank
ASA	Association for Social Advancement
BBS	Bangladesh Bureau of Statistics
BIDS	Bangladesh Institute of Development Studies
BRAC	Bangladesh Rural Advancement Committee
CDF	Credit Development Forum
GB	Grameen Bank
GOs	Government Organizations
GOB	Government of Bangladesh
GNI	Gross National Income
HDI	Human Development Index
IFPRI	International Food Policy Research Institute
IGVGD	Income Generation for Vulnerable Groups Development
IMFIs	Islamic Microfinance Institutes
InM	Institute of Microcredit
KMO	Kaiser- Meyer- Oklin
METRIS	Monitoring European Trends in Social Sciences and Humanities
MF	Microfinance
MFIs	Microfinance Institutes
MRA	Microfinance Regulatory Authority

NFPCSP	National Food Policy Capacity Strengthening Program
NGOs	Non-government Organizations
PBC	Perceived Behavioral Control
PBUH	Peace Be Upon Him
PKSF	Palli Karma-Sahayak Foundation
RDS	Rural Development Scheme
SACP	Special Agricultural Credit Program
SEM	Structural Equation Modeling
SNs	Subjective Norms
TPB	Theory of Planned Behavior
TRA	Theory of Reasoned Action
UNDP	United Nations Development Programs
WB	World Bank

Chapter 1

BACKGROUND: POVERTY ALLEVIATION AND MICROFINANCE

1.1. INTRODUCTION

Looking at the currently ongoing principles of microfinance institutes (MFIs) originated by the Grameen Bank model, the book attempts to identify the hurdles and prospects for improvement in microfinance model of development when considering why and how microfinance works and when and why it fails to achieve its original promise of poverty alleviation. Critically analyzing the unpleasant facts and figures of the 'one-size-fits-all' microfinance model (Islam, 2007) the book bridges the fissure between the claims that microfinance is a panacea for poverty alleviation and the opposite-claims that forewarn against such enthusiasm.

Taking the Grameen Bank (GB) of Bangladesh as a role model, this book explores the significance of shifting the focus of the model from a credit-led system to a client-led, flexible financial service providing scheme. Transforming into a client-led financial service scheme requires refocusing on clients, listening to their demands and preferences, and learning about their financial strategies (Islam, 2007). To this end in view, microfinance needs to be fundamentally re-examined focusing on the general attitude, intention and participation or nonparticipation behavior of poor clients of MFIs. In order to have a significant impact on poverty alleviation of poor clients, the entire industry must overcome all the bottlenecks that MFIs are presently facing. The time has come to reconsider the purpose, obstacles and potential of microfinance, going far beyond microloan for enterprise development to invigorate the provision of demand-led flexible financial services to poor people irrespective of whether they own enterprises (Islam, 2007).

The prime objective of this paper is to understand the role of MFIs in alleviating poverty along with their problems and prospects. In so doing, the study examines the intended participation and nonparticipation behavior of rural poor women collecting data from the "Four-Big" NGO-MFIs such as GB, Bangladesh Rural Advancement Committee (BRAC), Association for Social Advancement (ASA) and Proshika of Bangladesh.

Bangladesh is one of the world's most densely populated countries, with its people of 162 million crammed into a delta of rivers that empties into the Bay of Bengal. Poverty was deep and widespread, but Bangladesh has in recent years reduced population growth and improved health and education. GDP growth has climbed from less than 4% in the early 1970s to around 7% in 2015; per capita income has surged from less than US$ 100 in 1972 to US$ 1465 in FY2016; poverty has fallen from more than 83% in the early 1970s to 23.8% in 2015; fertility rate has decelerated from 7.3 in 1974 to 2.1 in 2014; life expectancy has increased from 55 years in 1974 to 69 years in 2017; child mortality has declined from 240 per thousand from 1974 to 31 in 2014; and adult literacy has increased from 22% to 64% over the same period. Bangladesh has achieved food self-sufficiency and the economy is transforming from an agrarian base toward a modern manufacturing and services economy. In 2015, Bangladesh crossed over from a World Bank classified low income economy to a lower middle income economy. And in the early 2018, Bangladesh termed it a historic day as it attained all three criteria for graduation from the least-developed country group to developing one. The UN Committee for Development Policy determines the graduation of a least developed country from the LDC category on the basis of its meeting at least two of the three criteria which are Per Capita GNI, Human Asset index (HAI) and Economic Vulnerability Index (EVI) (New Age, 2018).

Poverty is a one of the major problems in Bangladesh. Poverty is basically multidimensional in nature. It is referred to as unequal distribution in income, spectacular increases in the cost of living, malnutrition by the vast majority of the population, air and water pollution, unemployment and internal migration. Reasonably, thus, a major agenda of Bangladesh is to reduce poverty and increase rural employment for which the country has targeted a wide-ranging approach to poverty eradication, economic stability, trade liberalization, and setting up of various government and non-government organizations (NGOs). As such, significant advancement has been observed in realizing a conventional microfinance scheme (i.e., interest-based rather than Islamic microfinance) with a huge possibility for expansion (Ashraf, 2014). Thus, conventional microfinance whose subsequent term simply microfinance used in this treatise may have to shoulder more responsibilities in this environment because the government of Bangladesh has adopted it as one of the major tools for alleviating rural poverty and achieving other social agenda within a reasonable time frame (IMF, 2014).

The poor may not have any access to the formal credit market primarily because they are not considered to be credit worthy (Karim, 2011). As such they cannot have any credits from the banks or other financial institutions. Hence, they resort to the informal money market[1] including the village moneylenders who supply loans but charge exorbitant rates of interest. Microcredit is, thus, a small loan for the poor (ADB, 2012).

'Microcredit' or its subsequent version 'microfinance' (Elahi & Rahman, 2006; Hulme, 2000; Rutherford, 2003) has become a catchphrase since the early 1980s when Grameen Bank (GB) was established as a full-

[1] The informal money market includes friends and relatives, neighbors, shopkeepers and traditional money lenders (village *Mahajans* in local words).

fledged specialized rural bank in Bangladesh. A microfinance scheme primarily employs a broad range of monetary and financial services such as deposits, loans, utility bills services, money transfers, and insurance to poor, low income households and small businesses (ADB, 2012). The provision of small amounts of collateral-free formal loans to the poor for self-employment and income generation is an innovation of Grameen Bank (Ashraf, 2014). The Grameen Bank is now one of the leading microcredit service providers in Bangladesh.

The earliest reference to small loans goes to Jonathan Swift who inspired the Irish Loan Funds of the 18th century. However, the concept was widely known to the public when Dr. Muhammad Yunus, an Economics Professor of the University of Chittagong in Bangladesh and his Grameen Bank was awarded the Nobel Prize in 2006 (Ferdous & Uddin, 2010). Factually, the idea of 'microfinance' is the brainchild of Dr. Muhammad Yunus, who materialized his idea in 1976 into a revolutionary project initiated in a nearby village of Jobra (Yunus, 1976). Later, it turned into a rural development project integrated with new and revolutionary innovative features that radically overturned established ideas of the poor as clients of financial services and brought the rural poor especially women into its tiny network in order to build up microenterprises through only their own worth or skill in handicrafts fabricated out of cane, bamboo sticks, palm and date leaves (Yunus, 1997).

Microcredit was found to be a successful financial scheme, which disproved many traditional arguments such as the poor are not trustworthy because they do not have any asset to keep as collateral, and that women are not economically viable. In the process, it has broken the old concept that the poor are not bankable, generated a variety of lending methods, showing that it is possible to provide cost-effective financial services to the poor, mobilized millions of dollars of social investment for the poor and given rise to thousands of microfinance institutions (MFIs) dedicated to serving the very poor[2] in many countries all over the world (Woller, 2002).

---

[2] According to Grameen Bank's definition, the poor include the village peasants who possess not more than half acre of land including homestead areas. Other terms such as ultra-poor,

Besides Bangladesh, MFIs replicated on the Grameen model for their operations (Ashraf, 2011b) can now be found in Zambia (Copestake, Bhalotra, & Johnson, 2001), Zimbabwe (Barnes, Keogh, & Nemarundwe, 2001), Nigeria (Anyanwu, 2004), Nepal (Adhikary & Goldey, 2010), India (Mitra, 2009), Bolivia (Brett, 2006), Bosnia and Herzegovina (Hartarska & Nadolnyak, 2008), China (Park & Ren, 2001), Vietnam (Duong & Izumida, 2002), Malaysia (Ashraf, 2011a), Indonesia and in many other developed societies. The existence of the MFIs in these countries is evidence of the positive benefits rend ered by various MFIs.

1.2. Problem Statement

"Bangladesh has long been seen as the archetypal theatre of poverty" (Azam & Imai, 2009, p. 4). In reality, the history of poverty in the South Asian region dates back to the British Colonial history (Azam & Imai, 2009). However, the issue of poverty in Bangladesh arose just after its liberation in 1971 and it has become a central issue after the devastating famine in 1974 and which persists onward. Within the backdrop of acute poverty during 1970s, the microcredit approach was originated as a project in south-east Bangladesh in 1976 with a grand mission of alleviating poverty and raising the living standard of the rural areas. But, this approach gained credibility as a poverty-reducing tool in 1983 with a full-fledged license of the banking status of Grameen Bank (GB).

In Bangladesh, poverty has been recorded since the early 1970s. Evidence shows that the estimated poverty level was 82.90 percent in 1973-74 (Azam & Imai, 2009). Though this level has declined to a large extent in the 1980s, rural poverty (long after GB's initiative since 1983) was recorded at 36.0 percent in 2010 (involving 25% of the country's

---

poorest, extremely poor, hard-core poor and absolutely poor mean that these classes of people live below the poverty line by earning less than USD1.25 per day based on the World Bank's definition. The people of Bangladesh are mostly landless or marginally landless.

population) (World Bank, 2013). The trend of poverty in Bangladesh can be observed in Table 1.1.

Table 1.1. Poverty Trends in Bangladesh from 1973-74 to 2016

Year	National (%)	Urban (%)	Rural (%)	Poverty gap (%)	Squared poverty gap (%)
1973-74	82.9	81.2	93.0	NA	NA
1981-82	73.0	66.0	73.8	NA	NA
1983-84	52.3	40.9	53.8	15.0	5.9
1991-92	49.7	33.6	52.9	14.6	5.6
1995-96	53.1	35.0	56.7	15.5	5.7
2000	49.8	36.6	53.1	13.8	4.8
2005	40.0	28.4	43.8	9.8	3.1
2010	31.5	28.0	36.0	NA	NA
2016	24.3	18.9	26.4	NA	NA

Sources: BBS (1986); Azam & Imai (2009); World Bank (2013), CPD (2018), NA: Not available.

Table 1.1 shows that Bangladesh had a higher level of poverty in 1995/96 than that in 1983/84. In 2010 and 2016, the level of poverty decreased substantially (CPD, 2018). Interestingly, the poverty level in the rural areas decreased at a slower pace than the urban areas where no significant microfinance activities were observed (World Bank, 2013, CDF, 2017). It indicated that MFIs in Bangladesh did not play a substantial role in reducing rural poverty. This scenario highlights the unquestionable participation (or nonparticipation) of the poor in microfinance activities. In other words, this raises considerable doubt may arise about the status of the participation (or nonparticipation) of the rural poor in major NGO-MFIs including Grameen Bank in Bangladesh. Despite evidence indicating that MFIs are shown to be a highly successful tool to raise income and alleviate rural poverty (Hossain, 1984, 1985; Khan, 1990; Khandker, 2006; Khandker & Chowdhury, 1996; Khandker, Khalily & Khan, 1995; and many others), then why does poverty still persist in Bangladesh? What is the participation (or nonparticipation) level of the rural poor? What are the barriers to rural poor's nonparticipation in MFIs?

Evidence of participation and nonparticipation is available in a panel survey data which indicated that in 1998/99 of 60 million rural land-poor households in Bangladesh, 31.6 million (53%) participated in MFIs rural poor about, which means that 28.4 million or 47 percent did not participate (Khandker, 2006). Khandker (2006), however, did not inquire about why almost half of the rural poor did not participate nor whether they intended to participate in MFIs. Participation in MFIs is expected in Bangladesh because the global community acknowledges it as a potential development scheme to alleviate poverty (Imai & Azam, 2011). However, participation was not as expected. Statistics (see Table 1.2) provided by CDF (2017) and World Bank (2013), Daley-Harirs (2009) and Alamgir (2009) on microfinance participation in Bangladesh that revealed the level of participation and nonparticipation in MFIs during 2016/17 stand 5 million more than those provided by Khandker in 2006. It raises the question on why about 47 percent of the poor did not participate in the MFIs (see Table 1.2) in Bangladesh despite it being originated in the country and recognized by the global community (the Nobel Committee) as a successful poverty reducing tool.

Table 1.2. NGOs and Microfinance in Bangladesh up to 2009-2013

Organization category	Participants of rural poor (million)
NGOs	10.0
GB, ASA, BRAC, Proshika	18.0
BRDB-Bangladesh Rural Development Board (Government organization)	3.6
Total	31.6

Source: CDF (2017), World Bank (2013).

Table 1.3. Basic Statistics of NGO-MFIs in Bangladesh

Particulars	2010	2011	2012	2013	2014
Number of Licensed NGO-MFIs	516	576	590	649	676
Number of Branches	17,252	18,066	17,977	14,674	16,991
Number of Employees	109,597	111,828	108,654	110,734	114,644
Number of Clients (Million)	25.28	26.08	24.64	24.60	25.17
Number of Active Borrowers (Million)	19.21	20.65	19.31	19.27	19.98
Amount of Loan Outstanding (BDT Million)	145,023	173,798	211,283	257,010	278,017
Amount of Savings (BDT Million)	51,363	63,304	75,206	93,990	112,991

Source: MRA (2014).

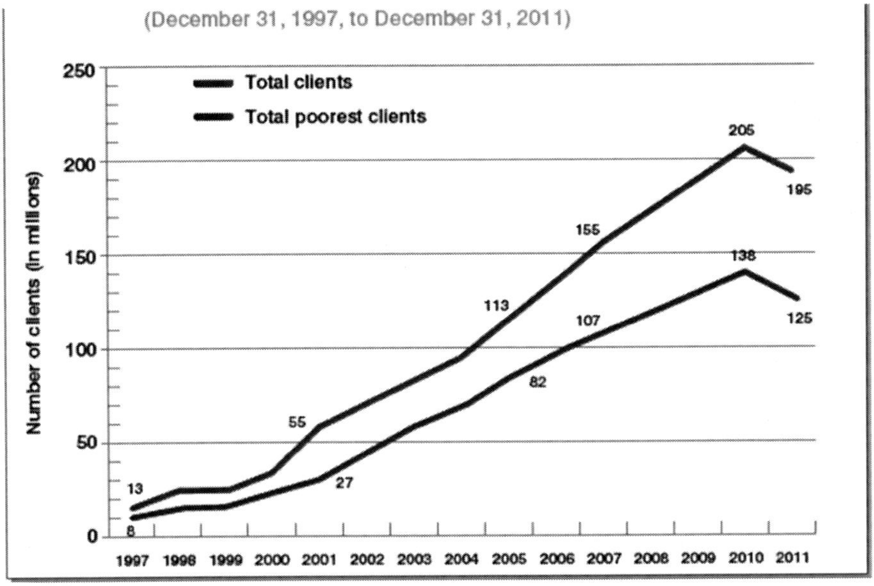

Source: Roodman (2013).

Figure 1.1. Growth of microfinance participation.

Interestingly, the statistics in Table 1.2 and Table 1.3 showed that the microfinance sector has almost saturated and it has not much growth in Bangladesh. Roodman (2013) reported on the state of saturation of microfinance throughout the world. He observed that in the first time in microfinance history, the number of microcredit borrowers fell sharply during the period from 1998 to 2011, as shown in Figure 1.1. According to his report (Roodman, 2013), most of the decline happened in India and Bangladesh, which attributed to a global decline in MFI participation.

If participation in MFIs is becoming stagnant, then it is vitally important to investigate the causes of this saturation or zero growth of participation in microfinance sector (Zohir, 2001) particularly when published research works on barriers to participation (or nonparticipation) in MFIs in Bangladesh are very limited (Ashraf, 2011c). Even if some published works are available, they are not empirical in nature. For instance, Evans, Adams, Mohammed, and Norris (1999) merely developed propositions that program- related and client-related factors influence nonparticipation in MFIs in Bangladesh. Their propositions, however, remain to be tested empirically. Zohir (2001), on the other hand, merely proposed that nonparticipation and participation of the rural poor in MFIs can be stratified into different groups: (a) those who never participated and never intended to participate; (b) those who intended to participate but lacked sufficient requirements like adequate resources and time; and (c) those who are currently participating

According to the report, most of the decline happened in India and Bangladesh. In this respect, Indian MF activist Vijayalakshmi Das refers that MFIs appear to be fragile, because they lost sight of their clients' interest and paid the price for which the things went wrong in India and Bangladesh and the global total number of microfinance borrowers fell. It indicates that the number of borrowers has been observed to reduce in these two countries. Based on this new evidence, it can be ratified that the participation of the rural poor in MFIs in Bangladesh is getting declined.

Nonetheless, nonparticipation of the rural poor in MFIs focusing particularly on its barriers is sparsely common and understudied. Though few researchers have undertaken some studies highlighting about nonparticipation and the impact of different socioeconomic parameters, there has been very little research that incorporates the intention of the poor in any theoretical model in their study in identifying the variables present in the model which can thwart the participation of the rural poor and their intended behavior (Ashraf, 2011c, Khandker, 2006; Evans, Adams, Mohammed & Norris, 1999).

To the best of the author's knowledge, there has been a study done by Ashraf (2011c) which investigates into factors of nonparticipation in MFIs. We postulate seven factors which are (i) lack of knowledge or education and (ii) individual experiences, (iii) religious value index and (iv) female head of household, (v) ill health, (vi) insufficiency of resources and (vii) entrepreneurial skill and training. However, we used single dimensional variable for measuring participation activity in his studies exploring nonparticipation of the rural poor in Bangladesh.

Similarly another published study is available done by Evans, Adams, Mohammed & Norris (1999) which explores factors of nonparticipation in MFIs in Bangladesh based on theoretical analysis. The study categorized factors in two groups: program-related and client-related. However, the study postulates its hypotheses theoretically and does not test any of them empirically. The study reveals that although three-quarters are eligible for microcredit, less than one-quarter take part in microfinance activities (NFPCSP, 2007).

In fact, the nonparticipation and participation of the rural poor in MFIs can be stratified into different dimensions such as the person (i) who never participated and never intended to participate, (ii) who intended to participate but lacked sufficient requirements like adequate resources and time and (iii) who are currently participating (Zohir, 2001). Yet, to the best of the author's knowledge, there are no such studies published that examine these types of behaviors of the rural poor in terms of microfinance participation or nonparticipation which can focus on the factors that affect poverty alleviation in society.

Finally, since nonparticipation in MFIs is a behavioral activity and a social phenomenon with a mixture of subjective and objective elements, any investigation on nonparticipation in MFIs remained incomplete if it does not take into account intention of human individuals and its antecedents (Ajzen & Fishbein, 2005). Hence, it is imperative to explore the reasons behind the low participation in MFIs in Bangladesh by adopting a behavioral theory that has been widely cited and applied extensively in the social psychological research (Abraham & Sheeran, 2003; Fen & Hong, 2009). A case study has been included in later part of this book testing the postulated factors of inhibiting participation of the rural poor in MFIs. The results of the experiment will be able to testify the arguments for the possible reasons of the dismal role of MFIs in poverty alleviation.

In the case study, it has been argued to be a suitable theoretical construct for the study of human behavior owing to number of rationales to predict various types of human behavior, which is the Theory of Planned Behavior (TPB) (Azjen, 1991) and contextualizing it in the context of the issue under study by incorporating several unique rural poor related factors often associated with nonparticipation in MFIs among the rural poor in Bangladesh. As the TPB model theorizes that intention is influenced by attitude, subjective norm and perceived behavioral control, the influence of these unique factors, to be referred to as the external factors, on the nonparticipation in MFIs should be viewed in terms on their effect on the three independent constructs of the TPB model.

1.3. RESEARCH QUESTIONS

As there is a considerable gap in previous research which investigates the reasons influencing intention and the participation behavior of the poor in microfinance institutions in Bangladesh, the present study outlines the research questions as to what extent can intention and nonparticipation or participation of the poor in MFIs be explained and also what are the factors that influence attitude, subjective norms (social pressure) and perceived behavioral control of the rural poor in MFIs in Bangladesh.

1.4. OBJECTIVES OF THE STUDY

The broad objective of the present study is to explore the factors that influence low participation of the poor in MFIs in Bangladesh which subsequently influences negatively on poverty alleviation. The specific objectives, on the other hand, are as follows:

1. To investigate the status of poverty alleviation through a theoretical model in explaining nonparticipation (or participation) in MFIs among the rural poor in Bangladesh;
2. To explore the factors that influence the attitude of the rural poor toward intended nonparticipation (or participation) in MFIs in Bangladesh;
3. To examine the factors that influence subjective norms of the rural poor toward intended nonparticipation (or participation) in MFIs in Bangladesh;

4. To analyze the factors that influence perceived behavioral control of the rural poor toward intended nonparticipation (or participation) in MFIs in Bangladesh.

1.5. SIGNIFICANCE OF THE STUDY

The particular contributions of this study are as follows:

1.5.1 Contribution to the Theory and the Body of Knowledge

In order to identify why there is low participation of the rural poor in MFIs, it is imperative to apply investigating tools that can help to expose the dynamics of the intention of human behavior. As human behavior is guided by different kinds of beliefs associated with socio-cultural norms, individual attitudes and behavioral control (Ajzen, 1991), the present research employed Theory of Planned Behavior (TPB) as an analytical tool. TPB has been used extensively in social psychological research to predict various types of human behavior; but, to date, this theory has not been used to explain microfinance participation or nonparticipation. As TPB's predictive ability in explaining human behavior has been consistently validated (Ajzen, 1985), it is expected that this theory will help discover the factors for the low participation of the rural poor in existing MFIs. In contextualizing TBP, this study considered socio-cultural background of Bangladesh as the potential factors that may affect nonparticipation of the rural poor in MFIs. In this respect, this study contributes to the theory by extending contextual variables which were not considered in previous works.

This study also contribute to the existing body of knowledge related to MFIs and literature on Islamic microfinance, which is a relatively new area of poverty-focused scheme, by discussing a holistic view of the microfinance sector operating in Bangladesh. In this respect, the analysis focuses on the possible alternatives of interest-based microfinance programs which seem to suffer from nonparticipation of the rural poor in MFIs in Bangladesh.

1.5.2 Practical/Policy Contribution

If the study can successfully identify why there is low participation of the rural poor in microcredit programs, it would assist the government in formulating a better public policy to alleviate rural poverty and hence raise the overall well-being of the poor. Rural poverty reduction is a serious concern due to the following reasons:

1. Poverty is widespread in Bangladesh where about half of the total population is living below poverty line with 80 percent in the rural areas (Ahmed, 2009).
2. Particularly in the northern areas of Bangladesh, there are seasonal famines called 'Monga'. The northern areas of Bangladesh are both economically depressed and ecologically vulnerable because it is prone to river erosion and frequent floods, low crop yields, poor infrastructure, high landlessness among households, low agricultural wages, and little employment opportunities outside agriculture (Mahmud, 2010). In these hunger-afflicted areas, only about a third of the poor households were found to be members of MFIs. The low rate of participation in this region compared to other regions in Bangladesh confirms the view that the poor households as well as the regional pockets of extreme poverty are by-passed by the regular microcredit programs (Mahmud, 2010). As a result, more than a third of these households adopt seasonal labor migration as a strategy to escape from the 'Monga' season, which extends from September to November.
3. A few empirical studies of this type are done by the MFIs themselves which are very program specific.

4. To the best of the researcher's knowledge, previous studies on participation and nonparticipation did not consider the qualitative aspects of human behavior.

1.6. Scope of the Study

The study covered six major rural areas of six divisions in Bangladesh where the majority of the NGO-MFIs including Islamic MFIs have been operating since the late 1970s. These areas were selected because MFIs have been in operation for a long time and the higher concentration of poverty (GoB, 2010). In this respect, these districts can represent the entire rural population of Bangladesh in helping us understand why there is low participation of the poor in MFIs in Bangladesh.

The study collected data from 280 nonparticipants and 140 participants in the six areas. To ensure a representative sample of the population and a normal curve of probability distribution, 420 data were deemed adequate (Hair et al., 2010).

1.7. Organization of the Study

The thesis is organized in six chapters which are as follows: Chapter 1 presents the background of the study which includes problem statement, research questions, objectives, significance and scope of the study. Chapter 2 delineates an overview of microfinance organizations in Bangladesh, their history and development. In Chapter 3, theoretical background and review of the relevant literatures are discussed. Chapter 4 explains the methodology adopted in achieving the objectives of the study. This chapter also elaborates the research framework and data analytical techniques. Chapter 5 discusses the study's results in detail along with their interpretations and implications. Chapter 6 concludes the study by summarizing the key findings and offering policy recommendations.

Chapter 2

EMERGENCE OF MICROFINANCE TO COMBAT POVERTY IN BANGLADESH

2.1. INTRODUCTION

Bangladesh became an independent country after a bloody liberation war in 1971. It is one of the tiny South Asian countries comprising the area of 143,998 square kilometers surrounded most of the land border by India from the east, west and north. But, Myanmar has a small border line in the south-east of Bangladesh. The Bay of Bengal is on the south of the country (Huq, 2001). This geographical location of the country makes it vulnerable to natural disasters. There are no such coastal regions in Bangladesh which had not been stricken by a cyclone or tidal bore.

Given the above circumstances combined with ineffective government initiatives, the country has been caught by a widespread poverty circle. Foreign donors come up with funds to ameliorate this acute poverty, resulting in NGO involvement in development activities. NGOs have thus emerged as significant development partners of the government working hand in hand in all spheres of development programs in Bangladesh since its independence (Ullah & Routray, 2003). In fact, the NGO movement has been in action in Bangladesh since right after the Liberation War when the humanity in this part of the world was in stern jeopardy. An NGO named the Bangladesh Rehabilitation Assistance Committee (BRAC) began its operation in Februrary1972 incepting a project for providing relief and rehabilitation to the refugees of the Liberation War. Soon after 1972, BRAC renamed itself as the Bangladesh Rural Advancement Committee in order to develop a framework for sustainable development through building the capacity of the rural poor. This organization is reputed to be the mother of all NGOs in Bangladesh (Ullah & Routray, 2003). Though BRAC has initiated its work as a multi-dimensional village development program, it switched to concentrate its focus on a target group approach of rural development based on its early experiences. The primary target group of BRAC is the landless and marginal landless poor (owning less than 0.5 acres of land) who survive just by selling their physical labors on a daily basis. Thus, since 1972 BRAC has been one of the oldest and presently longest NGO in the world serving the rural poor as its primary target group in order to alleviate rural poverty.

Another NGO named Proshika was established in 1976. Initially, it was the center of the Canadian University Services Overseas (CUSO) which provided volunteer social services in Bangladesh funded by the Canadian International Development Agency and the Canadian Public Contribution. Since then, Proshika has been providing services to the rural poor in order to alleviate rural poverty as well as to promote sustainable development in Bangladesh. In this process of development, ASA (Association of Social Advancement) was founded in Bangladesh in 1978. Since its establishment, ASA has tried to integrate social development (in health, education, nutrition, and sanitation) with the provision of credit, but in 1991 it was entirely transformed into a microfinance institute for lending microcredit only (Rutherford, 2009). ASA is regarded nowadays as one of the Big Four NGO-MFIs in Bangladesh.

2.2. MFIs in Bangladesh: An Overview

Bangladesh, a newly independent and war-ravaged country, had witnessed severe poverty since 1971 (Mahmud, 2010; Sen, 1982). Acute shortage of food owing to the destructive deluge in 1974 all over the country and some other global geo-political affairs were followed by large scale famine. Millions of inhabitants of the country became affected of that catastrophe. In order to overcome the effects of the catastrophe, the poor needed credits, but credit was hardly ever accessible to the poor victims to some of their assistance at affordable interest rates (Mahmud, 2010). Nationalized commercial banks also did not come forward to extend their credit facilities to meet the necessities of the poor (Ahmed, 2012) due to several reasons. First, commercial banks generally need collateral, which the poor failed to provide. Secondly, filling up application forms and fulfilling other official procedures for getting credit were too difficult for the uneducated poor and, lastly, the banks preferred to extend bigger volume of credit rather than small loans that the poor desired (Hossain, 1985).

In the situation of unavailability of rural credit facilities, the joint study of BIDS/IFPRI (1985) found that interest free loans provided to 40 percent of the poor came from informal sources (such as friends and relatives). The rest of the 60 percent poor, however, had to pay on average an interest charge of 125 percent per year even though the formal sources of lending charge on average was only at a rate of 14.6 percent per year. Thus, the only option left to the poor was to get loans from professional village moneylenders who are known as *mahajans* and wealthy farmers (Alamgir, 2009). About 92 percent of the absolute and marginal landless peasants relied on these loan sources, who charged exorbitant rates of interest (Hossain, 1985). This situation is called a market failure of the financial sector in Bangladesh. Against this backdrop, alternative measures were essential in achieving the goals of poverty alleviation and rural development.

Having observed the financial market failure, Muhammad Yunus conceptualized an innovative design of rural credit disbursement project in

1976. His primary aim was to help the rural poor escape from the exploitation of village moneylenders and to break the vicious circle of poverty (Yunus, 2001). With this end in mind, he initiated an action research project, called the "Grameen Bank Project - 1976" which came into being with the following objectives:

1. To extend the banking facilities to the poor men and women.
2. To eliminate the exploitation of the money lenders.
3. To create opportunities for self-employment for the vast unutilized and under-utilized manpower resources.
4. To bring the disadvantaged people within the framework of some organizational format which they can understand and operate and can find socio-political and economic strength through mutual support.
5. To reverse the age-old vicious circle of "low income, low savings, low investment" into an expanding system of "low income, credit, investment, more income, more credit, more investment, more income."

The Grameen project was experimented for three years in the Chittagong district. Then, the scheme was extended in the Tangail district in 1979 with financial support from the Central Bank. Until May 1980, there were 24 branches of Grameen project (19 in Tangail and five in Chittagong). The project found an excellent loan repayment rate of about 98 percent (Hossain, 1985). This experience was rarely found in other formal lending system in Bangladesh. The project subsequently included Patuakhali in south Bengal, Rangpur in north Bengal and Dhaka district in 1982. Within a short span of time, the project was able to include all other regions in Bangladesh and the then government acknowledged it as a full-fledged specialized rural bank in October 1983, which is now famously known as the Grameen (i.e., rural) Bank in Bangladesh.

In observing Muhammad Yunus's effort, Wahid (1996) states:

> "Muhammad Yunus made the village his classroom and started to understand 'the process of poverty'. Soon he realized that poor people were much more capable of taking care of themselves that was being portrayed in the traditional literature. He observed that the poor villagers, having virtually no asset, worked hard at a variety of crafts and service jobs and absence of any major shocks, could survive. Unfortunately, they could not accumulate any capital because of two reasons: first, their income was quite low and second, out of this income, after deducting for sustenance, whatever insignificant surplus they were generating was going to local money lenders from whom they borrowed small capital. The moneylenders were charging usury as high as 10 percent per month. This was one of the principal impediments for the villagers to get a head start. Thus if the poor villagers were to succeed, Yunus discovered that credit was the key" (p. 14).

2.2.1. Microcredit Development Stage in the 1980s

The Grameen Bank (GB) initiated its microcredit program to alleviate rural poverty and uplift the livelihood of the rural poor in Bangladesh with some innovative and special operational features. These features finally shaped the Grameen concept as a distinct type of model of poverty alleviation known to be the Grameen model of microcredit. The summary of these features are listed in Table 2.1.

As shown in Table 2.1, the Grameen Bank introduced a unique operational system of providing microcredit to the rural poor on a group-lending basis. Each group is comprised of five members who cannot be relatives, but known to each other. At first, only two members are allowed to have loans. Given the good performance of these two borrowers, the next two borrowers are permitted to take loans. Then, the fifth comes next to have the loans based on good performance of all those preceding four borrowers. The GB also provides training to the borrowers. The GB is composed of five office-layers ranging from the Head office to the Center office. The entire organizational arrangement of GB loan system and operations is shown in Figure 2.1.

Table 2.1. Summary of Grameen Model

Grameen concepts	Description
Borrowers	The rural poor who possess less than half-acre of land including homestead areas and their total wealth does not exceed the market value of one-acre of medium quality of land are eligible for borrowing money from the GB.
Members joined in groups	Grameen bank adopted unique loan systems that involve voluntary formation where people create groups. Each and every group consists of five members. Only two members are allowed to take a loan at the first time. If their performances reach a satisfactory level, then the next two borrowers can apply for loans. Finally, a fifth member can be selected for loan.
Loan size and repayment methods	GB's average loan size is USD75, except for housing loans. It charges a simple interest at a rate of 20% a year. Principal is repaid first, so that a borrower of USD75 would typically repay USD1.5 a week over 50 weeks. Interest, calculated weekly on the diminishing principal, is repaid only after the principal is paid off.
Meetings	Every GB center consists of eight groups or forty members who are required to attend the weekly meeting arranged by the center-manager. In these meetings, the members also repay their weekly loan installment along with necessary agenda on other issues.

Source: Shukran and Rahman (2011).

The Grameen Bank introduced a core of social agenda known as 16 decisions. These are actually recited by the members as slogans in a weekly meeting of the center which debuts with physical training and parade. The Garmeen Bank expects that all members follow these decisions in their daily life (Hossain, 1988). The 16 decisions are as follows: (i) We shall maintain unity, discipline, and hard work in daily life; (ii) We shall bring prosperity to our family, (iii) We shall not live in a dilapidated house; (iv) We shall construct tin-shade house and we shall grow vegetables year round; (v) We shall plant seedlings of trees during plantation season; (vi) We shall keep families small and look after our health; (vii) We shall send children to school; (viii) We shall keep our houses and environment clean; (ix) We shall have latrines in every home; (x) We shall drink water from tube-wells otherwise we shall boil drinking water; (xi) We shall arrange for dowry free marriages for sons and daughters; (xii) We shall not inflict any injustice to anyone, nor shall we allow to do so; (xiii) We shall undertake collective enterprises for raising incomes; (xiv) We shall cooperate with fellow members and help each other at difficult times; (xv) We shall not allow breach of discipline in any center; and (xvi) We shall do physical exercises and take part in collective social activities.

After the establishment of the GB in 1983, more MFIs later surfaced dedicated to rural finance and overall socio-economic development. In essence, the GB spurred a beacon of immense hope as an effective tool for eradicating rural poverty from society (Sengupta & Aubuchon, 2008). Though the terms microcredit and microfinance are often utilized interchangeably, there are important differences between the two. While microcredit refers to the provision of small loans to the rural poor, microfinance includes financial services in its program in addition to rendering merely microcredit alone. The financial services that are provided to the rural borrowers subsume the facilities of savings and securities as insurance for rainy days. In this sense, microfinance is a broader term which encompasses the field of microcredit (Sengupta & Aubuchon, 2008).

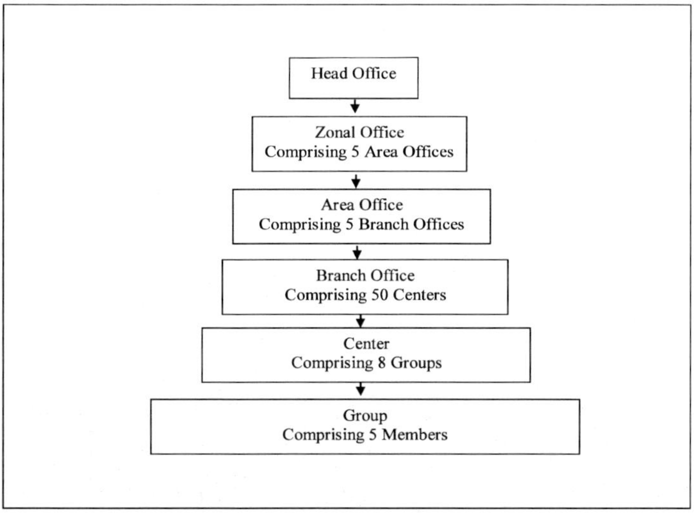

Figure 2.1. The Grameen Bank model of loan system and operations.

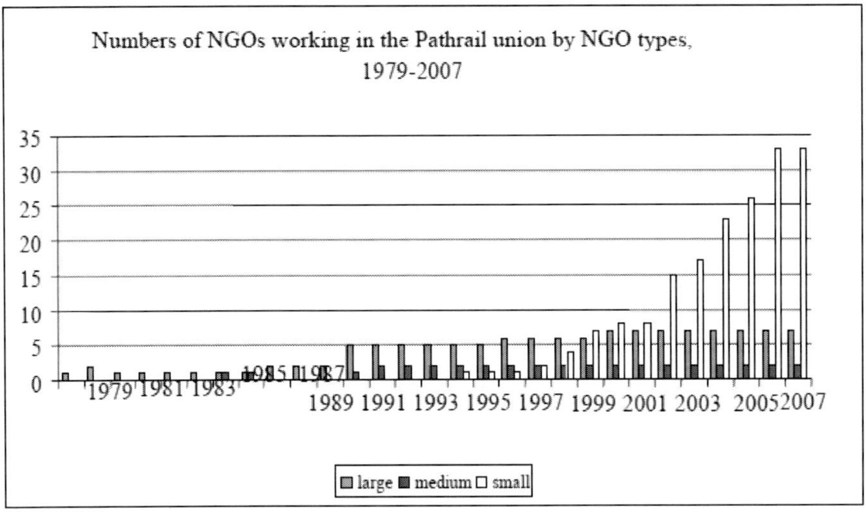

Source: Mahmoud et al. (2009).

Figure 2.2. Emergences of NGO-MFIs and their growth in 1979-2007.

It is evident that the growth of MFIs and NGOs for development was in surge through 1980s. Specifically many NGOs turned their operations focusing on the development of microfinance schemes (MRA, 2009; Pine, 2010). Following this path was the Caritas Bangladesh[3] that started micro-lending. However, due to massive loan defaults its microfinance program was terminated in 2010 (Caritas, Bangladesh, 2012). But there had been funds available on a large scale to be borrowed by the members of the MFIs for self-employment and generating more income. In this respect, a notable example is ASA which decided to solely operate microfinance programs in order to contribute to social and community development (Mahmoud, Khalily and Wadood, 2009; Pine, 2010). This new trend of NGO-MFI combination became popular among the NGO communities because they aspired be independent of the donors in terms of revolving loan funds. Once these revolving loan funds are borrowed by the target groups and then repaid, the funds become a real asset fully administered by the NGOs. In this way, NGOs found a solution to get away from total

[3] The Caritas Bangladesh is an NGO.

economic dependency on donor's aid and earn economic sustainability for itself (Huq, 2001). In this process, the bottom-poor, however, are excluded from the lending system because they are regarded by the NGOs as risky clients. The emergence and growth patterns of these NGO-MFIs are delineated in the Figure 2.2 which shows a fascinating growth pattern until the year of 2007. And after this time, microfinance faced critical time in terms of expansion of the participants in MFIs (Roodman, 2013).

2.2.2. Expansionary Stage in the 1990s

A remarkable growth in the number of MFIs was observed after 1990. Along with old institutions with new products of microcredit, new microcredit institutions came into the market with a significant potentiality that attracted attention of academicians, development practitioners and policy planners. MFIs in 1990s and onwards played a paramount role in massive expansion of this sector with its diversified microfinance products (Omoro, 2013). These MFIs have basically been contributing as development organizations, receiving funds and guidelines from domestic and international donors. Figure 2.3 shows the growth of MFIs in Bangladesh in the 1990s and 2000s.

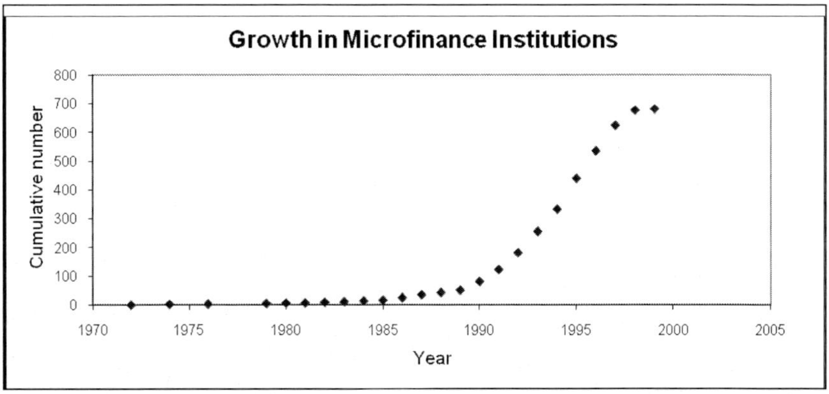

Source: Adopted from Rashid (2010).

Figure 2.3. Expansion of MFIs in the 1990s and 2000s in Bangladesh.

Table 2.2. Growth in No. of Branches of the Big-Four NGO-MFIs in Bangladesh

NGO-MFIs	Established	2004/05	2005/06	2006/07	2007/08	2008/09	2009/10
GB	1977	1,358	1,735	2,319	2,481	2,539	2,565
BRAC	1974	1,354	1,381	2,852	2,858	2852	NA
ASA	1991	1,965	2,291	2,496	3,303	3,324	3,194
Proshika	1994	191	195	213	NA	NA	NA

Source: MRA (2011) and GB (2011), NA = Not Available.

Bangladesh stands as the 8th largest country in the world in terms of its population (Hasan, 2008). About 50 percent of its population lives under the poverty line and 80 percent live in the rural areas (Pine, 2010). Given these facts, Bangladesh has a vast market for microfinance. Pine (2010) maintained that "the strategy of growth of MFIs was founded on a 'franchising approach', where new branches replicated the procedures of existing branches and offered primarily a standardized microcredit product to all clients making it easier to recruit new staff and train them quickly in a simple product" (p. 5). Following this policy approach, the MFIs were able to launch more branch offices at a quick pace in Bangladesh (Pine, 2010; Zaman, 2004). Not only the old NGOs, but many new MFIs were also launched to operate micro loans (MRA, 2010). Out of these MFIs, Big Four NGO-MFIs in Bangladesh namely BRAC, ASA, Proshika, and GB stand out. The growth of these Big Four NGO-MFIs in Bangladesh in terms of number of branches over the six financial years (2004/05 – 2009/10) is shown in Table 2.2.

In parallel to the growth patterns of the Big Four NGO-MFIs, the growth of cumulative disbursement of loans of the top NGO-MFIs in Bangladesh over the last five years are observed as shown in Figure 2.4. The total disbursement of BRAC and ASA is BDT1000 billion as of June 2011.

The Big Four MFIs and other NGO-MFIs provide their microfinance services to the rural poor based on the model of Grameen Bank that follows a group-lending approach in which emphasis is given particularly to women borrowers, weekly meetings and repayment of installment of loans. Table 2.3 presents the different sizes of NGO-MFIs in Bangladesh (Pine, 2010).

Table 2.3. Types of NGO-MFIs and Their Market Share in June 2013

NGO-MFI Type	Range of borrowers	No. of MFIs	No. of clients	No. of borrowers	No. of employ-ees	Loan outstanding (BDT mil)	Savings (BDT mil)
Big Four	More than 1 million	4	16,103,056	11,959,193	56,563	91,706.30	32,561.25
Large	0.1 to 1 million	21	3,962,855	3,962,855	3,962,855	3,962,855	3,962,855
Medium	10000 to 0.1 million	115	4,142,141	3,244,888	23,465	24,575.01	24,575.01
Small	Less than 10000	341	1,238,087	935,661	8,281	5,897.96	2,414.77

Source: MRA (2010); BDT = Bangladesh Taka.

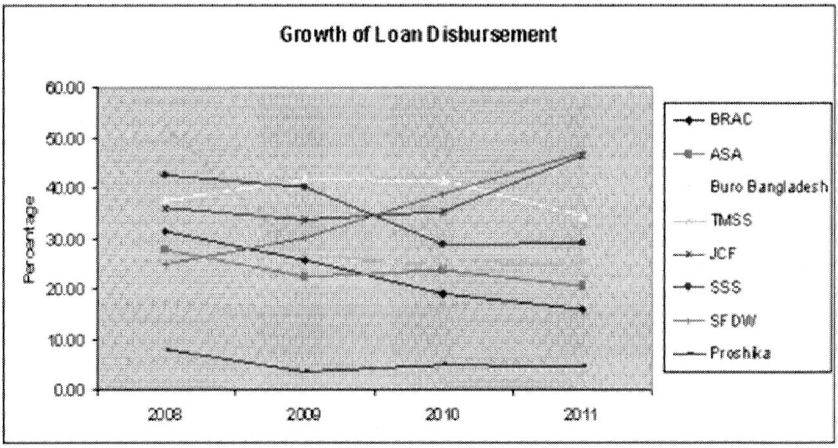

Source: Adopted from MRA (2011).

Figure 2.4. Cumulative loan disbursements of the top NGO-MFIs in Bangladesh.

Another development in the field of microfinance practices and their supervisions concerns with the formation of a supreme supervisory body named the Palli Karma-Sahayak Foundation (PKSF) which was founded in

1990. The PKSF is tasked to monitor all activities of the MFIs in the country. It is funded partially by the World Bank and partially by the government of Bangladesh. With the help of this organization, the growth of the MFIs has accelerated all over the country. The PKSF also helps manage the institutional infrastructure to reduce outreach, improve efficiency, increase self-sufficiency and reduce dependence on donor funds (Pine, 2010; PKSF 2009). In essence, PKSF plays an important role in increasing new members of the MFIs.

2.2.3. NGO-MFIs' Augmented Competition and Development from 2000 Onwards

NGO-MFIs have augmented their competition and development since 2000. The loan recovery performance came under crisis in the microfinance sector in Bangladesh loomed at the end of 1990s. Having such crisis, GB's loan repayment rates reduced from 98 percent to 90 percent (Armendariz & Morduch, 2005; Pine, 2010). This crisis was primarily due to the explosive growth of the Big Four MFIs such as GB, BRAC, ASA and Proshika (see Table 2.2) which increased their competition in providing loans. Consequently, the microfinance market experienced over-lending and overlapping of loans. In order to tackle this problem, the GB went back to scan its system of loan operations and tried to reformulate a more lenient microfinance lending toward the poor in a dynamic competitive financial market in Bangladesh (Pine, 2010). Not only the GB initiated this process, but other MFIs also reviewed their positions and changed their strategies in offering a wider range of products and services in order to avoid the crisis of microfinance in the credit market of Bangladesh (Pine, 2010).

Since the inception of NGO-MFIs in 1970s, there had been no microfinance regulatory authority (MRA) in Bangladesh until 2006. With an intense competition in microfinance sector in the late 1990s, MFIs experienced less availability of funding opportunities from the donors. In this new situation, several MFIs launched providing the services of voluntary and open access savings accounts to their clients. For this reason, the practitioners and policy makers in microfinance sector felt to impose regulation in the microfinance practices in Bangladesh (Conroy & McGuire, 2000; Pine, 2010).

Since the inception of NGO-MFIs in 1970s, there had been no microfinance regulatory authority (MRA) in Bangladesh until 2006. With an intense competition in microfinance sector in the late 1990s, MFIs experienced less availability of funding opportunities from donors. In this new situation, several MFIs launched voluntary and open access savings accounts to their clients. For this reason, the practitioners and policy makers in the microfinance sector felt the need to impose regulation (Conroy & McGuire, 2000; Pine, 2010). Following this concern, the Government of Bangladesh approved an "Act of Microcredit Regulation Authority" through which Microcredit Regulatory Authority (MRA) came into being in 2006. This organization had later approved a regulatory framework that became mandatory for all NGO-MFIs that have microfinance operations in Bangladesh (MRA, 2009). So, since 2006, MRA has been discharged for implementing the Act and monitor all the practices of microfinance lending activities of all NGO-MFIs. One of the most important regulations implemented by MRA was the imposition of the interest rate ceiling charged by the MFIs. By the rule, this rate was fixed at no more than 27 percent per annum. However, experts said that this rate was still considerably high and unaffordable for the poor clients of MFIs (Rahman, 2010). Lila Rashid, the Director of MRA, suggested that a balanced and affordable interest rate should be determined by justice and could be dispensed for the borrowers as well as the MFIs (Ferdous & Uddin, 2010).

Another important development in this period was the establishment of microfinance programs modeled against the Grameen Bank all over the world. The Grameen model has been replicated in 105 countries of the world including Bolivia, Chile, China, Malaysia, Ethiopia, Nigeria, Ghana, Indonesia, Honduras, India, Afghanistan, Mali, the Philippines, Sri Lanka, Tanzania, Thailand, the United States, Mexico, Vietnam and others (Sengupta & Aubuchon, 2008). But despite the GB's success, there have been growing concerns about the GB's achievements over three decades. The success of the GB as a poverty alleviating institute involves the inclusion of the poor rural women who constitute over 95 percent of its membership. However, concern about the deliberate exclusion of the poorest from its poverty alleviation scheme is a hot issue among the researchers and development practitioners nowadays. As such, there is a mixed opinion about the GB's scheme of poverty alleviation both at the household and the macroeconomic level (Amin & Sheikh, 2011). In fact, the GB's credit alone approach in supplementing the earning of self-employed beneficiaries does not help in any basic shifts in employment opportunities; it rarely generates new employment for others.

A recent report published by the Center of Global Development provided evidence of the dramatic fall of microfinance clients globally from 2011 particularly in India and Bangladesh (Roodman, 2013). The report suggests the saturation of MFIs in Bangladesh since early 2011. If the situation is indeed true, it is certainly alarming for the global community who aims to reduce poverty through microfinance. Finding a better alternative of microfinance programs is needed. One way this can be done is through Islamic-based microfinance initiatives. However, such tool has already been available since early 1990s where a few Islamic microfinance institutes as an alternative poverty alleviating tool to regular interest-based MFIs in Bangladesh have emerged (Ahmed, 2012). As a stakeholder in the microfinance market, the Islamic paradigm of interest-free MFIs deserves a special dedication. What follows is a brief discussion on Islamic microfinance institutions (IMFIs).

2.2.4. The Emergence of Islamic Microfinance Institutes (IMFIs) in Bangladesh

The emergence of Islamic microfinance institutions (IMFIs) in Bangladesh is an important event in the financial market. Interestingly, both Islamic banking and interest-based MFIs were established concomitantly in the mid-1970s (Ahmed, 2012). As one of the first countries to adopt microfinance, Bangladesh introduced Islamic microfinance in the early 1990s. While regular or interest-based MFIs have spawned their operations during the last three decades, the initiatives of poverty-focused and interest-free Islamic MFIs are still lagging much behind (Ahmed, 2004). But many IMFIs exist to assist in eradicating rural poverty. Leading Islamic microfinance organizations include the Rural Development Scheme (RDS), Al-Fallah, Noble, and Rescue. Background information of these four IMFIs is provided in Table 2.4. Among them, the RDS is the youngest in terms of the year of establishment.

Table 2.4. Basic Data on IMFIs in Bangladesh

	Al-Falah	Rescue	Noble	RDS
Local operation	Dinajpur	Rangpur	Bogra	Bangladesh
Year of establishment	1989	1991	1993	1995
Number of employees	212	74	20	2,363
Female borrowers (percent of total)	98.6%	97.5%	67.7%	85%
Drop-out rate (percent of total)	NA	3.8%	3.7%	NA

Source: Ahmed, 2002 and MRA, 2010; NA = Not available.

Because commercial banks exclude the poor from borrowing because they do not have sufficient physical collateral, the MFIs came into the picture to help them financially. Group-based dynamics of regular or interest-based MFIs act as social collateral and diminish the asymmetric information dilemma that hinders financial intermediation. Operationally, IMFIs used to practice in different way in terms of credit disbursement to overcome the asymmetric information and moral hazards. Like regular interest-based MFIs, IMFIs do not extend any loan in cash. They purchased the things and sell it to the clients on a mark-up basis. In this way, the clients cannot divert the funds to other purpose for which they primarily take the loans. In addition to this, the concerned officers of IMFIs used to closely monitor the clients' activities and also provide necessary advice to engage the funds in a profitable way. Therefore, there has been a less chance of losing money and also a less chance of being default to pay back the loans. Even though the IMFIs are still in a transitional stage which requires financial innovation based on Islamic values, they are fundamentally different from the interest-based MFIs in many ideological issues (Ali, 2012). The difference between Islamic MFIs and interest-based MFIs are shown in Table 2.5.

Table 2.5. Distinctions between Interest-Based Conventional MFIs and Islamic MFIs

	Interest-based MFIs	Islamic MFIs (IMFIs)
Assets (mode of financing)	Interest-based	Islamic financial instruments
Dealing with default	Group/center pressure threat	Group/center/spouse guarantee and Islamic ethics
Deductions at inception of contract	Part of the funds deducted at inception	No deductions at inception
Financing the poorest	Poorest are left out	Poorest are included by integrating *zakah* with MF
Funds transfer	Cash given	Goods transferred
Liabilities (sources of funds)	External funds, savings of clients	External funds, savings of clients, Islamic charitable sources
Liability of the loan	Recipient	Recipient and spouse
Objective of targeting women	Empowerment of women	Ease of availability
Social development scheme	Secular (or un-Islamic) behavioral, ethical, and social development.	Religious (includes behavior, ethics, and social)
Target group	Women	Family
Work incentive of employees	Monetary	Monetary and religious

Source: Ahmed (2002).

Table 2.5 represents a general comparison between interest-base regular MFIs and IMFIs. In fact, Bangladesh is the first country to introduce Islamic microfinance in 1989. Unlike interest-based MFIs, the financial instruments of IMFIs are predominantly *murabaha* (mark up sale) and *bi-mu'ajjal* (deferred sale contract) based on group-lending principles. IMFIs have thus evolved in this manner from *qard-al hasan* (interest free loans) structures (Mannan, 2010).

2.3. Performance of the IMFIs in Bangladesh

Evidence suggests that the overall performance of IMFIs is comparatively better than regular interest-based NGO-MFIs in Bangladesh (Mannan, 2010). In this regard, the case of the Rural Development Scheme (RDS), a sister concern of the Islamic Bank Bangladesh Limited (IBBL) can be mentioned. RDS started its operations in the mid- 1990s, whereas GB and BRAC were established in 1983 and 1972, respectively. However, the performance of RDS is much better than the performance of GB and BRAC in terms of specific indicators. In particular, the number of borrowers RDS has grown in comparison to other NGO-MFIs, which have seen a stagnant or decline (Roodman, 2013). Table 2.6 compares the performance of RDS, GB and BRAC.

Microfinance, with the growing popularity in Bangladesh, has been in existence for the last three decades, yet the change and shifts in terms of poverty alleviation and better lifestyle is still low. Evidently a majority of the population is still under the poverty line and many still do not have access to healthcare, sanitation, safe drinking water and basic nutrition. This chapter provided an overview of the MFIs in Bangladesh along with their growth patterns including Islamic MFIs (IMFIs). Specifically, it elaborated the environment in which the GB emerged, its basic features, scale of operation, modes and practices of other microfinance programs, coverage of financial services as well as the extent of poverty alleviation. In parallel to regular MFIs, it also discussed the emergence, trends and growth patterns of IMFIs as well. The distinguishing features of IMFIs are also delineated beside the conventional MFIs. Evidence suggests that Islamic MFIs are going ahead quite fast, with a growth rate of more than 10 percent (Mannan, 2010).

Table 2.6. Performance of RDS, GB and BRAC (1997-2012)

Areas of Performance	RDS	GB	BRAC
Year of establishment	1995	1983	1972
District covered	61	64	64
Recovery rate	99.58%	96.88	98
Investment growth	12.57%	6.7	7
Drop-out rate	5%	15	8
Member per branch	3439	3262	1893

Source: Islamic Bank Bangladesh Limited (IBBL) (2012).

Chapter 3

THEORY AND PAST RESEARCH: POVERTY ALLEVIATION THROUGH MICROFINANCE PROGRAMS

3.1. INTRODUCTION

The Grameen Bank (GB), Bangladesh Rural Advancement Committee (BRAC) Association for Social Advancement (ASA), Proshika and many other NGO-MFIs have been well-studied in terms of their program design as a rural financial intermediary and their association with the poor men and women in rural areas of Bangladesh. There have also been critical studies on outreach, and exclusion and nonparticipation of the rural poor that ultimately hinder the efforts of poverty alleviation in the rural areas of different parts of the world including Bangladesh.

3.2. THEORY AND CONSTRUCTS

The present study employs the theory of planned behavior (TPB) as its theoretical background based on which the analytical framework has been formulated. As mentioned earlier, the study postulated several factors to impact on the original variables of the theoretical base of TPB in order to predict about the participation and nonparticipation behavior of rural poor women in the conventional MFIs in Bangladesh. In so doing, the study explores different constructs of the analytical model based on previous empirical literature in the following sections.

3.3. THEORETICAL MODEL

This chapter explores the theoretical model of nonparticipation in MFIs in Bangladesh. It also sheds light into the concepts of intention toward nonparticipation, attitude, subjective norms and perceived behavioral control (PBC). The model forms a foundation upon which the research framework and methodology are based. Theory-based research is important for several reasons (Knabe, 2012). Theories guide scholars and provide hints about the direction of research for protecting researchers from the mistakes made in day-to-day inquiry (Babbie, 2001). Theories offer scholars models and paradigms in order to explain the social world. Using independent variables and dependent variables to represent a theory's constructs, researchers can test theories in different studies, advancing the scientific understanding within different disciplines (Knabe, 2012).

The ultimate goal of a scientific discipline is the development of theory or hypothesis that results into valid and meaningful predictions about phenomena not yet observed (Chalmers, 2013). Hence, a theoretical model is the structure that can hold or support a theory of a research study. Theoretical underpinnings based on the postulates and hypotheses developed in different contexts can lead to an effective way to be fully engaged in the research topic (Friedman, 1953). In this sense, a theoretical model is designed to explain the reality or to predict about certain behavior (Sinclair, 2007). Thus, theoretical models are an important tool of advancing theories and aiding decision makers for further policy options (Cooper & Schindler, 2006, Kennedy, 2008).

A growing and increasingly important trend in the social sciences is to think about scientific inquiry and attempt to understand specific research problems from an interdisciplinary perspective (METRIS, 2009). One way to do this is not to rely exclusively on the theories in a particular class, but to think about how an issue might be informed by theories developed in other disciplines (METRIS, 2009). In this study, Theory of Planned Behavior (TPB) (see Figure 3.1) was employed as a theoretical background because it has a wide range of implications and diversified perspectives of human behavior. TPB is a popular theoretical model that extended Theory of Reasoned Action (TRA) (Fishbein & Ajzen 1975) by adding a concept of perceived behavioral control (PBC) because the latter has limiting ability in explaining intended behaviors in which a person does not have volitional control over it (Ajzen, 2008). TPB describes how people's behavior can be determined by their intention to perform a certain behavior (Ajzen, 1985, 1988, 1995, 2006, 2008).

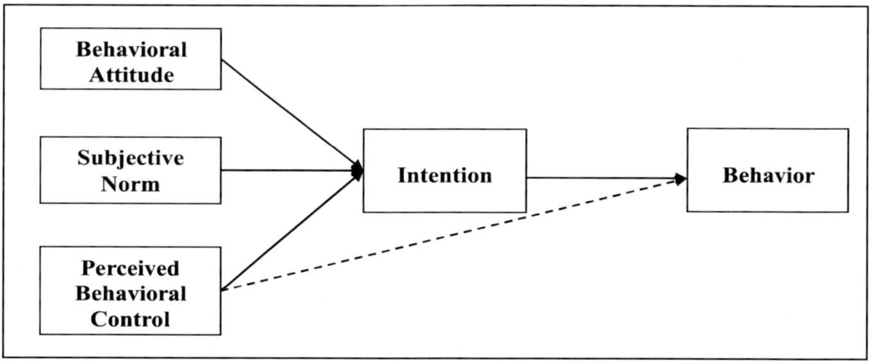

Source: Ajzen (1991).

Figure 3.1. Conceptual model of the theory of planned behavior (TPB).

TPB puts forward that immediate antecedent of actual behavior is intention of someone to involve in that behavior. Intention encompasses behavioral motivations to perform the behavior (Ajzen, 1991). Attitude and subjective norm affect actual behavior through the variable of intention.

According to Ajzen (1991), attitudes are in general individual judgment to engage in a specific behavior, but subjective norms are the social enforcement on an individual to engage or not to engage in that behavior. In addition to attitudes and subjective norms, TPB intends to predict some behaviors which are not fully volitional by employing perceived behavioral control (PBC) over engagement in the behavior as an extra domination of intention and behavior (Ajzen, 1991). PBC is the perceived idea of easiness or complexity in engaging in the behavior and has been idealized to apprehend the apparent behavioral skills or abilities, resources and opportunities (Ajzen, 1991). The following explains further the TPB constructs of intention, attitude, subjective norm and PBC.

3.3.1. Intention

In TPB, intentions are regarded as the immediate antecedents to an actual behavior and correspond to the blending of the cognitive, motivational and affective interior course of actions connected with a given behavior. Intention is, thus, measured as the best predictor of a deliberate human behavior (Ajzen, 2006). Ajzen and Fisbein (2000) maintained that intention isthe hub of the theory. They put forward that someone becomes inclined to be engaged in an actual behavior whenever any opportunity comes up and as the person's intention is stronger than others, s/he is more likely to perform that behavior. TPB advocates intention as a function of three variable-components such as attitudes toward the behavior, subjective norms, and perceived control over the behavior.

3.3.2. Attitude

Attitude toward the behavior in question is considered to influence intention and it is the least controversial construct in TPB (Armiatge & Conner, 2001). Attitudes are defined as either *instrumental*, which is one's perception of the usefulness of the behavior, or *experiential* attitudes which are described as a one's positive or negative feeling toward the behavior (Ajzen, 2006). TPB mainly concerns with a comprehensive attitude construct which operationally characterizes two distinct affective (e.g., fear) and instrumental (e.g., individual preference as beneficial or harmful) attitudinal constructs (Rhodes et al., 2006).

Empirically, there are supports for these two distinct independent constructs to represent the behavioral assessment which is observed consistent in TPB research and attitude research more generally (Ajzen & Driver, 1991). Support was also found in different research contexts and settings such as in product marketing (Lam & Hsu, 2006; March & Woodside, 2005; Mohsin, 2005). Their findings suggest that cognitive decision-making process of human behavior is influenced by the experiences regarding any particular preferences attained during the past daily life. Other studies investigated the direction of the causal relationship between attitudes and behavior (Anker, Feely & Kim, 2010; Kaiser & Schultz, 2009; Mason & Cheyne, 2000; Smith et al. 2008; Suhayati, 2012). Their findings suggest that attitude had a causal impact on behavior. However, according to Fishbein and Ajzen (1975) attitude may influence behavior indirectly mediating through the variable of intention which intuitively encourages utilizing the research framework of TPB. Yet, there are evidences which show that attitude has a positive relationship with intention to behavior (Bergkvist, 2009; Okun & Sloane, 2002).

Research on attitudes toward microfinance participation embedded particularly in TPB construct is scanty. However, there have been numerous attitudinal researches on the participation of workers in political or voting activity (Ekstein, Noack, & Gniewosz, 2013; Zini, 2002). Among several factors, attitudes toward politics were found to be significantly and independently associated with workers' political activity (Hewlett, 2008). Other researchers demonstrated that attitude toward any activity was one of the best predictors of participation and willingness to participate (Allen, 2011; Neidhart, 2005; Rice, 2011; Stout, 2012; Zini, 2002).

3.3.3. Subjective Norm

The second major concept of the TPB model is subjective norm which is closely related to intention to predict actual human behavior. Normative beliefs are related to subjective norms about how other fellow-citizens associated with a person would evaluate him/her for performing the behavior. This behavior can be participation in certain activities or inhibiting certain activities (Armitage & Conner, 2001). Ajzen (1991) maintained that several social referents have a dominant influence on someone's decision making process. Hence, the more a person realizes how other social pressure groups think an individual ought to perform a specific behavior, the more likely that the person is likely to perform the behavior (Lee, 2011). Indeed according to Lee (2011), even though the relationship between subjective norms and intention toward certain behavior appears to be reasonable, the degree of influence depends on how much individuals value the advice given by their referents. These social pressure groups include socio-political and religious leaders, teachers and co-workers in addition to family members and friends or relatives.

Recent findings indicate that, among others, subjective norms led to formation of intention to perform a behavior (Delaney, 2009; Gavaza, 2010; Jefferson, 2012; Moon, 2011; Payton, 2011; Philips, 2009). That is, a person's family, spouse, peers, coworkers, partners, social, religious and political leaders were found to influence an individual's decisions to participate in an activity.

Perceived Behavioral Control (PBC)

Perceived behavioral control (PBC) is an additional construct incorporated into TPB. The inclusion of PBC to TRA in addition to its two original constructs of attitude and subjective norms to influence intention toward the targeted behavior was made due to TRA's inability to deal with behavior over which an individual has incomplete volitional control

(George, 2004). According to TPB, not all behaviors are completely under volitional control and are instead contingent to either outside assistance or interference. Such was the fundamental argument for adding the component of perceived behavioral control, in an effort to account for external forces (von Linden, 2010). Perceived behavioral control (PBC) thus refers to the degree of control that an individual perceives over performing the behavior (Chen, 2007; Kang et al., 2006; Zini, 2002). According to Ajzen (2001), PBC is defined as the extent to which a person feels able to engage in the behavior. In other words, perceived control is the self-assessment of both the capability or skill and the opportunity to perform the behavior. Positive attitudes, social approval, self-efficacy and decisional autonomy come together to strengthen the intention and the chances of performing a behavior (Casper, 2007).

According to Ajzen (1991), the importance of control on actual behavior is self-evident. Any behavioral achievement must depend upon the availability of required resources and relevant opportunities to involve in any activity. Hence, PBC plays an important role in TPB. This is due the fact that if any activity is not within complete control of someone, then s/he fails to take part in that activity. It could be due to lack of necessary resources or time which are the precondition to perform that specific behavior. In this regard, Ashraf (2014) demonstrated that many people in the rural areas of Bangladesh did not participate in microfinance programs because they did not possess necessary resources and time to do so.

This study identifies various potential factors hypothesized to be potential barriers to participation (nonparticipation) in MFIs in line with TPB model. These factors are associated with attitude, subjective norms and perceived behavioral control regarded as antecedents of intention toward participation. As TPB is an extension of TRA and both are used to evaluate the intentional behavior of participation (nonparticipation) (Sommer, 2011), it would be useful to compare the two models to maintain the rationale for using TPB rather than TRA.

3.4. Rationale for the Adoption of the TPB Framework

Empirically, TRA was found to have some limitations in predicting human behavior (Ajzen, 1991; Kaiser & Gutcher, 2003; Lee, 2011). In predicting human behavior sufficiently, it is, thus, imperative to look for other alternatives such as those provided by several scholars (e.g., Greenslade & White, 2005; Lemmens et al., 2005). However, TPB is considered to be the most appropriate in this regard (Sommer, 2011).

According to several scholars (Armitage & Christian, 2003; Biddle & Nigg, 2000; Courneya & Bobick, 2000; Fen & Hong, 2009; George, 2004; Rivis & Sheeran, 2003), TPB model exhibits the most applied and suitable theoretical construct for the study of human behavior owing to number of rationale as follows: (a) TPB was found to represent the most convincing and well-established model for the prediction of intentional human behavior; (b) the theory has been shown to effectively work under a wide variety of circumstances and in various disciplines such as social psychology (Albarracin, Johnson, Fishbein, & Muellerleile, 2001), community attitudes and market research (Ajzen, 2008), political participation (Avery, 2007; Gaeke, 2009; McCormick, 2009), sports science (Chatzisarantis & Haggar, 2008), nursing and healthcare workers (Munday & Silk, 2008), health medicine (Hyde & White, 2009), communication (Zhou, 2007), driving behaviors (Elliott, Armitage, & Baughan, 2007), smoking behavior (Brann & Suttan, 2009; Wang 2009), romantic relationships (Jang & Woo, 2009), organ donation (Siegel et al., 2008) and information technology (Armitage & Conner, 1999; Ashraf, Alam & Noor, 2010; Notani, 1998); (c) TPB is a parsimonious theoretical framework, which involves relatively a small number of variables that can accurately predict actual human behavior. Thus, any study that intends to analyze human behavior, TPB is the most appropriate theoretical framework which is based on personal, social and individual control toward intention to actual behavior (Fen and Hong, 2009). Besides, any theoretical model that identifies multidimensional factors in influencing human intentional behavior based on cognitive, social and psychological aspects is more desirable (Biddle & Nigg, 2000; Symons, Downs & Hausenblas, 2003) than a model that does not have such features.

Fourth, TPB offers an organized course of action and plainly defines the construct or framework that could help researchers determine social cognitive perception to attain greater predictive accuracy (Ajzen & Fishbein 1980). In this regard, Ajzen (2008) refers to the utility of associating the limiting conditions remained within the TPB framework that is compatible. Besides, the methods and guidelines that are useful in constructing the TPB questionnaire can be easily retrieved from online resources. Thus, it can be conferred that the TPB framework is beneficial to attain the dual goals of a theory such as the explanation and the prediction of a given behavioral activity that employs behavioral intention as a mediating variable (Sommer, 2011).

The fifth reason, according to Ajzen (1991, is that general dispositions tend to be a poor predictor of behavior in specific situations. Empirical relations between general traits and behavior in specific situations are found to be low. If this relationship is considered between other personality traits and specific context, the outcomes become more disappointing (Ajzen, 1988, 2008). As the present study deals with specific contexts predicting specific behavior like participation of the rural poor in MFIs, TPB can produce more valid results than other theoretical frameworks.

Abraham and Sheeran (2003, p. 265, as cited in Fen & Hong, 2009) noted that "as a model of the cognitive antecedents of behavior, TPB is parsimonious, empirically supported and can be operationalized easily, according to available guidelines." Still, the dominant flow of the cutting edge research along with this quotation can provide significant support for using TPB as a theoretical framework in predicting a specific behavior (Gaeke, 2009). Thus, the TPB model is more suitable and inclusive in predicting human behavior than TRA (Chen et al., 2009; Fen & Hong, 2009). This argument is particularly relevant for microfinance participation of the rural poor who frequently face time, financial and social security constraints (Evans et al., 1999). Hence, by considering the control factor over behavior that possibly influences individuals' intention to participate in any activity (Casper, 2007), TPB is reckoned to be more valid than TRA that focuses on attitude and subjective norms only.

3.5. Nonparticipation in MFIs

Studies on nonparticipation of the rural poor in MFIs that focus particularly on barriers are sparse. This is true not only in Bangladesh, but also globally. However, a few researchers in Bangladesh have undertaken some studies on nonparticipation and its impact of different socioeconomic parameters. Yet, very little research on the barriers and obstacles of participation of the rural poor in MFIs has been conducted (Ashraf, 2011c, Evans et al., 1999; Khandker, 2006), and on the factors that potentially influence nonparticipation of the rural poor in MFIs in Bangladesh.

Evidence of participation (nonparticipation) is available in a panel survey data which indicated that in the early 2000s about 53 percent (i.e., 47% nonparticipants) of total rural land-poor households in Bangladesh participated in MFIs (Khandker, 2006). This study, however, did not inquire about the reasons for which almost half of the rural poor were not participating nor intended to participate in MFIs. Recently Razzaque (2010) and Sen and Hulme (2006) observed that the Big Four MFIs gave out loans to about only 19 million people when almost a quarter of population live in extreme poverty. It was further observed that the level of microfinance participation and nonparticipation in MFIs provided earlier by Khandker (2006) was similar to that observed in later years (Alamgir, 2009; Daley-Harris, 2009; World Bank, 2013) (see Table 1.2). These studies demonstrated that the microfinance sector appears to be saturated with no possible growth. Indeed, a dramatic fall of microfinance clients seems to be a global phenomenon since 2011, as indicated in a recent report published by the Center of Global Development (Roodman, 2013). Roodman (2013) described that for the first time in 2011, the number of microcredit borrowers fell sharply. According to the report, most of the decline happened in India and also some in Bangladesh. The report also showed that MFIs appeared to be fragile because their clients' lost interest in microfinance borrowing.

The above evidence indicates a decline in participation of the rural poor in MFIs worldwide. Even though microfinance has been recognized as an important poverty reduction tool, it begs questions as to why there is a decline in participation of the rural poor such as in Bangladesh. Hence, studies that aim to help explain this situation are timely and justified (Zohir, 2001). However, published works on the reasons for nonparticipation in MFIs in Bangladesh are very scarce (Ashraf, 2011c). Even if there are any, they have some limitations. For example, Evans et al. (1999) proposed factors of nonparticipation in MFIs in Bangladesh and categorized them into two groups: program-related and client-related. No empirical data were collected. In a different study, Ashraf (2011c) investigated the factors of nonparticipation in MFIs by incorporating TPB as its theoretical base in Bangladesh. However, in his study, he did not incorporate intention as a precedent of nonparticipation. He postulated seven factors that influence nonparticipation. They were lack of knowledge or education and individual experiences (as antecedents of attitude); religious value index and female head of household (as antecedents of subjective norms); and poor health, insufficiency of resources and entrepreneurial skill and training (as antecedents of PBC). Even though SEM was used as the analytical tool, he did not employ factor analysis to identify the underlying dimensions of the postulated factors. He treated nonparticipation as a uni-dimensional variable.

3.5.1. Intention toward Nonparticipation in MFIs

Literature recognizes the importance of intention in explaining human behavior. This conveys the message of the volitional and purposive nature of human activity (Huq, 2001). Intention is treated as antecedent of actual behavior in the TPB model. In this respect, Ajzen and Fishbein (2000) put forward that intention plays a central part of theory of planned behavior and plays an important role as a direct antecedent of a behavioral construct. They argue that when an opportunity is available, the stronger the intention is and the more likely the behavior will be performed (Lee, 2011). Ajzen and Fishbein (2000) continued that the links between intention and performing the behavior has been practically investigated in a closed environment. In this regard, they assert that the relationship between the two variables is difficult to measure in reality because there are numerous external factors that can influence the relationship. Consequently, substantial part of the research has highlighted on behavioral intention rather than actual behavior. In this regard, Ajzen and Fishbein (2000) expounded that behavioral intention is presumed to predict actual behavior (Lee, 2011).

In relation to the field of microfinance, there are limited studies that investigate the rural poor's intention to participate (or not participate) in MFIs. As intention of the individuals to take part in microfinance programs depends on different factors such as the judgments of eligible households about the costs and benefits of taking part and the influences of social and cultural subjects (Ashraf, 2011c), the present study incorporated intention as an antecedent of participation (nonparticipation) of the rural poor in MFIs.

3.5.2. Attitude toward Intended Nonparticipation in MFIs

Among the three antecedents of behavioral intention, attitude toward behavioral intention has been widely investigated in various fields such as in anthropology (Galani-Moutafi, 2000) and social psychology (Stedman, 2002). Generally, attitude focuses on an individual's preference in choosing a particular behavioral action. Ajzen and Fishbein (1980) traced the origin of using attitude in social behavioral studies. They found various works that attempted to define and explain what attitude is. However, even though Fishbein and Ajzen (1975) asserted that attitude does not exclusively predict behavior, it could predict behavior much more accurately than any other single variable.

Ajzen (1991) defined attitude as "to the degree to which a person has a favorable or unfavorable evaluation or appraisal of the behavior in question" (p.188). Attitudinal behavior of an individual person focuses on the ultimate consequences of the behavior and her/his overall assessment of the pertinent outcome. In fact, attitude toward a behavior can lead to the formation of a behavioral intention (Ajzen, 1991).

Jansen and Pippard (1998) studied the Grameen Bank in Bangladesh as a model of microenterprise development by focusing on women's attitudes toward economic and social development needs. They used content analysis in describing gender inequities in participation as a background for understanding the importance of Grameen Bank for poor women in the rural Bangladesh. They found positive attitudes of women's toward participation in microfinance provided by the bank.

3.5.3. Subjective Norms toward Intended Nonparticipation in MFIs

Subjective norms are contingent on normative believes and motivation reinforced by the people important to the individual person in performing a particular behavior (Fu, Richards, Hughes & Jones, 2010; Manning, 2011). According to Ajzen (1991, p. 188), subjective norms is "the perceived social pressure to perform or not to perform the behavior." As a person's subjective norms are influenced by someone's opinion, intention toward certain behavior is formed conjointly. Subjective perception of an individual about the normative surrounding together with attitude can predict intention (Fishbein & Ajzen, 1975).

In the case of participation (or nonparticipation), some influential personalities can motivate the rural poor to participate or not to participate in microfinance programs. In this context, family friends, spouse, relatives, religious leaders can have a strong influence on the formation of intention of an individual (Armitage & Christian, 2003). Ashta and de Selva (2012) reviewed the relationship between religious practices and microfinance participation behavior. They asserted that people who wish to benefit from micro-credit are mostly the poor and their success in business is linked to religious behavior. They also recognized that the interactions between microfinance and other fields of the society such as religion have received little coverage, even though religious institutions often play an important role in setting microfinance systems and their consequences. As conventional MFIs basically operate on interest which is forbidden in Islam, religious leaders can influence the rural poor not to participate in the microfinance activities (Dusuki, 2008; Ashta & de Selva, 2012). As the religious leaders also demand that women wear a veil or cover in the presence of male adults who are not *muhrams*[4], such imposition often appears to be a barrier for women to take part in microfinance borrowing activities (Dutta & Magableh, 2006).

3.5.4. PBC toward Intended Nonparticipation in MFIs

According to Ajzen (1991), the importance of control on actual behavior is self-evident. Thus, any behavioral achievement must depend upon the availability of required resources and relevant opportunities. PBC plays an important role in TPB because if any activity is not within complete control of someone, which may be due to lack of necessary resources or time, then s/he fails to take part in that activity. Hence control is the precondition to perform a specific behavior. In this regard, Evans et al. (1999) demonstrated that many people in the rural areas of Bangladesh did not participate in microfinance programs because they did not possess the necessary resources and time to do so.

---

[4] Muhram is an Arabic word. It means the male persons who are forbidden by Islamic religious law to marry a particular woman.

3.6. FACTORS OF NONPARTICIPATION IN MFIS

The original construct of the theory of planned behavior consists of three independent variables such as attitudes toward behavior, subjective norms and perceived behavioral control. However, Ajzen (1991) asserted that if there are other potential factors that could predict particular intention and behavior better, then the model could be extended. Thus, TPB is in fact open to include predictors that can capture a significant influence on intentions as well as on actual behavior. Based on this premise, variables incorporated in the present research are fear of risk associated with loans, individual preferences, religious restrictions, spousal dislike for female being the head of household, friend's influence, insufficiency of resources, lack of knowledge and poor health. These variables are postulated to improve predictions of microfinance intention and participation (or nonparticipation). In so doing, we modified the TPB model by incorporating these factors in order to explain the barriers of participation (or nonparticipation) in microfinance institutions in Bangladesh. In the next section, we discuss the relevant literature on the factors mentioned above.

3.6.1. Fear of Risk Associated with Loans

Some people avoid risk associated with dangerous activities because of fear. According to Lockwood (2011), for many, fear is experienced when they consider the negative outcomes they could experience as a result of entering into risky situations. Thus, fear associated with risk ought to be considered when investigating nonparticipation of the rural poor in MFIs.

The term 'risk' is believed to be originated in the Middle Ages and was related to maritime insurance to the difficulties one could face at sea (Breivik, 2007). In reality, conventional contemporary conceptions and usages of the term 'risk' are rooted in early economic theory, where risk is defined in utility theory and relates to the estimates of the likelihood and magnitude of potential costs and benefits. However, more recent approaches to the study of risk acknowledge the limitations to this approach and almost exclusively focus on perceptions of loss, cost, harm or other terms used to denote negative consequences (Breivik, 2007). Extensive debates concerning this issue are not the primary focus of the current research. The main focus here is on the relevance of risk in relation to the people's motivations to participate or not participate in microfinance schemes (Mukherji & Wright, 2002). As such, risk in this study is interpreted as either the judgments of uncertainty that people make about any potential harmful outcomes of their nonparticipation and/or those potentially harmful outcomes. In behavioral theory, a number of contextual variables are integral to the decision-making process. These contextual variables include aspirations and expectations as well as income stream variability or risk (Mukherji & Wright, 2002).

Fear of risk associated with loans stems from several incidents that happened in rural Bangladesh. Rahman (1999) cites cases where the workers of the NGO-MFIs detained village-women borrowers and members if they missed to pay the weekly installments. In some extreme cases, the workers of the NGO-MFIs seized the household-assets of the poor borrowers including the wooden pillars and tin-roof of the houses for missing the installment of the loans. Rahman (1999) also mentioned that many rural poor members of the NGO-MFIs used to pay the installment of the loans by borrowing from other formal and informal sources. By doing so, a vicious circle of overlapping loans and poor economic outcome was created. All these instances shaped negatively the rural poor's attitudes toward participation in MFIs in Bangladesh.

Harassment is a critical social element experienced by citizens of contemporary Bangladesh (Dyal-Chand, 2007). Similar stories of harassment were reported in the PPRC (Power and Participation Research Center) Governance Survey (2006). The survey explored the analytical content of the harassment experienced by the poor and reported a significant range of misconduct from the NGOs and MFIs. As an instance of harassment, the residents of Arampur in northern Bangladesh reported stories such as physical abuse of borrowers in the hands of MFI officials. Unauthorized repossession of assets, including even the roof of the house of a loan recipient, frequently happened when borrowers missed their installments (Ferdous & Uddin, 2010). Added to this fact, one resident complained, "They use many kinds of force to get their money back ... torturing people or dragging people out of their homes .... it is a serious injustice. If we tell them we can't pay an installment because we needed money for treatment of our children, the field officer grouch" (Ferdous & Uddin, 2010, p. 40). It appears that microfinance puts more emphasis on loan repayment than helping the recipients fix their life. Instead of empowering individuals and communities, repayment creates an environment of fear and intimidation where recipients must regularly sacrifice basic needs to meet an inflexible repayment schedule.

In the case of arrears and default, Rahman (1999) reported similar disturbing stories more than a decade before. He found in his study that conventional MFIs used to utilize group and center pressure to force the borrowers to make repayments of their loans. When the peer pressure failed to produce the weekly installment of the loans, sometimes threats from the MFIs were followed and in extreme cases assets of the poor borrowers were sold by the MFIs to repaying the loans. As a result, many rural poor lost all of their scanty belongings including houses and small home-lands (Karim, 2011). Rahman (2009) also reported that as a result of these harassments, the poor did not trust the NGO-MFIs in meeting their economic expectation, which resulted in economic insecurity and mental anxiety.

Dyal-Chand (2007) compared two modern examples of human worth as collateralization that were at geographical, economic and cultural extremes. The first occurred in the context of credit lending to consumers in the United States. The second occurred in micro-lending programs used widely in developing countries as a means of economic development of the poor. The first involved, according to her, middle class people in the First World and the second example involved impoverished women in the third world. In so doing, she asserted that the two socio-cultural settings could not be more distinct; yet in both cases human worth had taken on a new role as a market asset, which was the subject of quantification, collateralization and diminution. The findings of her study are many-fold, as follows: First, certain characteristics of human worth consistently materialized when it serves as collateral. In both contexts, it is hierarchical, utilitarian and broadly distributive. Thus, it appears that human worth is not just collateralized in the two settings, but also that it is, in a sense, consolidated. Second, in both cases, the law has failed to recognize this new use of human worth. For example, in Bangladesh, the GB uses no court enforcement at all, relying exclusively on peer pressure to enforce repayment. So the lenders are structuring an extremely effective market for credit without the aid of laws that should be directly applicable. Third, in solving asymmetric information problem, both cases use a new kind of collateral out of a mechanism that was meant to solve moral hazards. In the United States, the lenders use, apart from the legal stance, the power of threat to the borrowers. In Bangladesh, the GB uses the power of social humiliation or *ijjat*. The final observation is that the credit market, more than the law, is operating as the carrier of norms about things as fundamental as human worth. The provocative of this point is that the market is playing a governing role in terms of nonparticipation that rule-of-law aspect to be played by government, legal, and other experts. There is microfinance regulatory authority to monitor any mismanagement in the microfinance program operations, but the government is inactive in implementing the regulations deemed by the regulatory authority.

Evans et al. (1999) undertook a study with the objectives to determine what differentiates the poor participating in MF initiatives from those nonparticipating and to which extent do risk factors and transaction costs affect participation of the rural poor. The study identified lack of female education, small household size and landlessness as risk factors for nonparticipation. They also reported that although three-quarters were eligible for microcredit, less than one-quarter took part in microfinance activities. They postulated several hypotheses in two groups in terms of program-related and client-related barriers, but hardly tested those hypotheses directly. Moreover, Evans et al. (1999) did not examine additional variables crucial in determining nonparticipation of the rural poor in microcredit programs in the present socio-economic conditions of

Bangladesh, such as the cost of credit, religious restrictions and loan repayment policy.

Mitra (2009) studied qualitatively the microfinance interest rates in India. The study argued that the field of microfinance emerged in the developing world as a vehicle to provide financial services to poor segments of population but which is gradually being shifted as a profitable business opportunity. The study used secondary data of several microfinance programs initiated by Citigroup, Merrill Lynch, Morgan Stanley, Deutsche Bank and ICIC and focused on the methodologies of calculating the flat interest rate followed by the MFIs in India. The study found that the word “flat” was being used by microcredit programs to mislead illiterate borrowers into paying a high interest rate on the pretext of providing social services.

According to Ferdous and Uddin (2010), as MFIs began to mature, they started facing performance dilemma, and the focus was gradually shifted toward profitability. In order to improve profitability, MFIs kept an interest rate on loan at a very high level and imposed additional costs in the form of margin money, compulsory savings and insurance premium to borrowers. Majority of MFI borrowers are poor and illiterate and they do not understand the financial jargons used by MFIs and their effective cost. To help the poor to understand the true cost of loan, MFIs should disclose effective interest rate to the then. Hiding effective interest rate by using “creative” accounting practices is highly unethical. Many MFIs simply state that they charge only 15 percent flat rate of interest. But the effective interest rate including processing fee, compulsory savings, etc. goes well over 100 percent per annum (Ferdous & Uddin, 2010). Karim (2011) found that the poorest perceived a loan to be too risky. Owning little asset and fearing about heavy responsibility of debt, they were reluctant to participate in MFIs. When taking a loan, they could fall into difficulty if the rate of the revenue from their investment fell short of the total cost of borrowing. According to Banerjee (1999), the gap between total revenue and total cost was then compensated by one of five choices: taking loans from local moneylenders; utilizing prior savings or selling properties; cutting off existing consumption expenditure; negotiating to reschedule the loans; or simply defaulting. According to Banerjee, some defaults, in turn, energized a demonstration spiral and many households practice self-exclusion.

Rahman (1999) reviewed extensive literature on microfinance programs that are supposed to help with sustainable development in Bangladesh. Yet, his anthropological investigation on the Grameen Bank demonstrated that bank employees were supposed to boost distribution of loans among their members and pushed for high recovery rates to earn profit necessary for economic viability of the institution. In order to make certain loans are paid back timely, bank workers and borrowing peers imposed extreme demands on women clients. In this regard, many borrowers used to maintain their regular repayment schedules through a process of loan recycling which considerably increased the debt-liability on the individual households, increased tension and frustration among household members, produced new forms of dominance over women and increased violence in society. Rahman also mentioned that this type of apprehension was widespread in the rural society of Bangladesh where people appeared to be reluctant to be member of any MFIs. Thus, fear appears to be potential barrier to the rural poor participation (or nonparticipation) in MFIs in Bangladesh.

3.6.2. Individual Preferences toward Intended Nonparticipation in MFIs

Another antecedent of attitude toward intention to participation (or nonparticipation) in MFIs in this study is individual preferences. According to Schiffman and Kanuk (2000), preference is the power or ability to choose one thing over another with the anticipation that the choice will result in greater satisfaction, greater capability or improved performance. Individual preferences may affect attitudes, which account for significantly more of the variance in individuals' desires or preferences than intention or self-prediction (Armitage & Conner, 2001). Ajzen (2007) referred personal desirability or preferences toward a behavior as the degree to which performance of the behavior could positively or negatively value.

Individual preferences and participation were examined by Jackson's (2005, 1988) studies which found that barriers included only one particular constraint such as any intervention that inhibited participation in any activities. According to Jackson (2005), the term barrier referred mainly to external individual constraints that intervened on the relationship between preference for an activity and actual participation. Past research indicated that negative signals or threatening events had negative effects that had a clearly adaptive function. These adaptive actions included ways to avoid, escape, or overcome the threatening events and efforts made to change the routines and the set of decision rules. These action preferences would be associated with negative signals regarding low organizational resources and inferior performance, as well as the negative framing of problems (Mukherji & Wright, 2002). Thus, individual preferences could lead to participation (or nonparticipation) of the rural poor in MFIs.

The original Grameen approach was to lend to individual borrowers in the village by forming loan groups. In this program, the individual was kept in line by a considerable amount of pressure from the other members of the group. The group and the loan center in this system function as institutions to ensure mutual accountability. The peer pressure along with the institutional and moral coercion that bank workers in the village exercise on women borrowers helped the local branch of the MFIs achieve and maintain 98 percent repayment rate (Mukherji & Wright, 2002). However, such peer-pressure and institutional coercion on women also produced unintended consequences for the borrowers and their households (Rahman, 1999), which shaped the rural women's preference and hence attitudes toward participation (or nonparticipation) in MFIs in Bangladesh.

In another study, Menon (2006) investigated the presence of individual preference of consuming different paddy crops among the rural poor. Data were collected from rural Bangladesh in three rounds of three different seasons of paddy crops. The sample was drawn from 24 villages of eight sub-districts where only the Grameen Bank was operating micro-lending operation. These villages were selected because the microcredit scheme had been in operations for at least three years. Participants and nonparticipants among the target households were separately identified and interviewed. Of 420 target households, 297 were participants. The length of membership was measured by the number of years the participants had been a member of the Grameen Bank. Menon found that although participation had a mitigating effect on seasonal shocks to consumption, the magnitude of such effects begins to diminish over time. Estimates from the model suggested that the effects reached a maximum at two years of membership and began to decline thereafter. This did not imply that consumption volatility increased for experienced members; it merely suggested that participation no longer had the same mitigating influences as before. The findings further showed that returns of the members to participation began to diminish after about two years of membership. This implied that membership alone no longer had a mitigating marginal effect on seasonal shocks to per capita consumption after four years of participation.

Finally, the debate about whether to lend to individuals or lend to groups was an important issue. The microfinance programs, which originated in Bangladesh, primarily operated in group lending where individual preference did not play any role in determining how the loans were used in individual entrepreneurial activities. Thus, getting a loan on an individual basis may pose a serious problem (Townsend, 2003). In this respect, Evans et al. (1999) asserted that nonparticipation might simply be a function of individual or household preferences that deemed credit as something that was not in their best interest. These preferences could change the participants' and nonparticipants' attitude toward intending to become members of the MFIs (Ajzen, 1991).

Studies that looked at individual preferences to participation (or nonparticipation) in a microcredit program also considered gender difference. For example, Khandker, Koolwal and Sinha (2008) examined participation in group-based credit programs by young women aged 15-30. They found that young women had a higher preference for credit than older women. They also compared the young women's participation with two other groups: older women (31 and older) and men residing in the households. They observed that the young women's borrowing was statistically significantly different from that of men's borrowing but not different from that of older women. However, the marginal returns to program participation were significantly higher for younger women than older women.

Weiss and Montgomery (2005) surveyed the evidence from Asia and Latin America on three issues such as the success of microfinance programs in reaching (i.e., participation of) the poor, the effectiveness of microfinance initiatives in pulling households out of poverty and the cost-effectiveness of microfinance as a poverty targeting tool. Based on available secondary information and content analysis, they suggested that whilst microfinance clearly might have positive impacts on poverty, it was unlikely to be a simple panacea for reaching the rural poor in the study areas.

3.6.3. Religious Restrictions

Religion is a system of beliefs and practices by which a group of people interprets and responds to what they feel is sacred (Kahf, 2004). Most religion prescribes or prohibits certain behavior including economic, financial and entrepreneurial behavior. Kahf (2004) also asserted that members of different religious groups are likely to use religious identity and instructions to make business decisions.

The rural society of Bangladesh is built in local networks in which religion takes a prominent place because around 87 percent of the population is Muslim (BBS, 2011) and Islam is the state religion in Bangladesh. Around 90 percent of the laws in Bangladesh are secular. So, there are legal problems in Bangladesh arising from unresolved conflicts in the law. For example, MFIs offer an alternative finance by providing microcredit and primary training to poor women. However, women independence or women empowerment program is against the beliefs of many strict Muslims (Ahmad, 2009) especially in the beginning when their activities were seen as undermining the traditional social and religious values of the country. Indeed, *The Economist* (2000) found that women violating *purdah* (females' physical exposure without any headscarf and extra clothes) by joining an interest-based microcredit program had been strongly condemned by religious leaders, who attacked the microcredit institutions because of their interest-based operations. Similar evidence was presented by Ahmad (2009), who found that many husbands did not allow their wives to join NGOs for fear of backlash from religious leaders. Hence, religious value is also another reason for participation (or nonparticipation) in a predominantly Muslim country like Bangladesh. In this context, religious values reflect the subjective norms of the TPB framework.

The role of religion in socio-economic development has also been examined by Ahmed (2012). In particular, he investigated the organizational models of Islamic microfinance. He demonstrated that religion played an important role in varying relative socioeconomic status of women and family behaviors across different religious groups. Similar finding was reported by Ali (2012). His data suggested that much of the variation in the relative socioeconomic status of women was due to differences in family behavior, and there was little evidence for the declining influence of religion in family behavior or in the socioeconomic inequality of women. He concluded that religious view on the status of women was a factor for nonparticipation in MFIs in Bangladesh. In the realm of *zakat*, Bidin (2008) explored *zakat* compliance behavior among Muslim employees. He used theory of planned behavior which incorporated religious values as a predictor of intention to pay *zakat.* He found that religious values influenced significantly whether employees comply with *zakat* payment or not.

Yousuf, Rahman and Shapin (2006) assessed the possibility of a mosque institution in Kelantan in running a microcredit program based on the group lending model of the Grameen Bank but on a small scale. Series of interviews with the managing director of Amanah Ikhtiar Malaysia and 10 Kelantan regional branch managers were carried out to explore their views regarding the issue. They found that more than 90 percent of the respondents believed that the mosque could run the group lending program because it possessed two strong foundations – the mosque committee members know the people within the local distance very well, and they had diversified experience to support the program. The respondents also stressed that the mosque administration has to spell out explicitly proper borrower targets, closely monitor the borrower's project, and strictly stay away from politics. The study concluded that religious institutions may be used for implementing a microfinance scheme in society but it should be in line with the Islamic principles in order to alleviate rural poverty. In Islam, interest is strictly forbidden. Using this religious principle, religious leaders discourage people not to participate in any financial activity that involves interest. They also cite the importance of maintaining women modesty in dissuading women to participate in the microcredit program.

3.6.4. Spousal Dislike of Female Head of Households

TPB postulates subjective norm as social pressure on individuals to perform or not to perform actual behavior (Ajzen, 1991). Subjective norm is considered to be a function of salient normative beliefs. While subjective norm relates to perceptions of *general* social pressure, the underlying normative beliefs are concerned with the likelihood that specific individuals or groups (referents) with whom the individual is motivated to comply will approve or disapprove of the behavior (Armitage & Conner, 2001). Spouse is considered one of the important social referents in the TPB framework (Ajzen, 1985).

As cited elsewhere, the majority of the borrowers of conventional MFIs are women (Karim, 2011). The objective of targeting women is to empower them (Ali, 2012). This is because women use the funds efficiently to increase their income levels. As a result, they will theoretically become more independent and gain self-respect. Zaman (2004) maintained that microcredit reduced women vulnerability by allowing them to raise income and consumption and building asset. Wahid (1999) observed a high proportion of women participation in the Grameen Banks microcredit program in relation to the proportion of women in the overall population of the nation. He attributed the high participation level to social factors such as demonstration effects, diminishing influence of village leaders, exposure of the society to the rest of the world, spread of education in the villages, and rising expectations about the GB.

Kabir (2001) observed that microfinance programs have been touted as a prominent tool in poverty reduction exercises in Bangladesh. One of the main targets of these programs is females from the poorest sections of the population. However, there are growing debates whether these programs actually benefit women in reducing reduce poverty or have made them worsened off. Recent studies showed that despite the objective of empowering women, microcredit program was shown to have an opposite effect (Karim, 2011). The women are usually persuaded by the male members of the household to obtain credit and utilize it. But, the women still have to bear the responsibility of repaying the loan because they are primarily the borrowers. This has generated chaos and conflicts in the family. Indeed, in the context of Bangladesh, empowerment of women could be deemed on the patriarchal socioeconomic background, defined by Cain, Khanum and Nahar (1979, pp. 405) as a "set of social relations with a material base that enables men to dominate women." Hence, it could be thought of as an improvement in intra-household gender relations (Hashemi, Schuler, & Riley, 1996). Ferdous and Uddin (2010) observed that while women were meant to be the primary targets of MFIs, they were more often the conduits of credits, not end-users. In this context, one villager was reported to have said, "Women take loans because their husbands ask them to do so. In most cases, failure to repay is not their fault but because their husbands either squandered the money or lost it in a wrong investment. Instead of being empowered these women are like chilies crushed between the mortar and the pestle. On one side, their husbands put pressure on them. On the other side, MFIs chase them for being loan defaulters" (pp. 43).

Similar observation was made by Buvinic and Gupta (1997). They noted that the female-head households were experiencing socioeconomic disadvantages which ranged from economic discrimination to social stigmatization and isolation that hindered their capability to meet the requirements for participating in microcredit schemes. In many cases, they found that the spouses of the female members of the MFIs did not like their wife to be the chief of the household. Even though Littlefield and Rosenberg (2004) contended that microfinance plays a crucial role in women empowerment by contributing in household income and assets, they noted that "microfinance alone is not a magic solution that will propel all of the poor – particularly the very poorest people — out of poverty (p. 40)." Rahman (1999) noted that women even though the microcredit programs encourage economic freedom for women to be heads of the household, this situation was blamed as a catalyst for family disintegration in rural Bangladesh. The negative effect of women participation is further exacerbated by the imposition of *purdah* by the male spouses as required by Islam, which may act as an important reason for nonparticipation of the rural poor in MFIs (Mahmud, 1994).

3.6.5. Friends' Advice on Nonparticipation in MFIs

Another important referent is friends who influence others either to be or not to be involved in specific activities (Ajzen, 1985). White and Wellington (2009) used theory of planned behavior to predict intentions to participate in group parenting education. Their analyses supported the role of self-identity and group norm in significantly predicting intentions. They also found that friends were significant referents that prevented individuals from participating in the parenting education programs.

Stories about how women experienced difficulties because they were not able to repay their loans had convinced close relatives and friends that participation would not benefit the women borrowers. According to Dyal-Chand (2007), women are more vulnerable than men in society, where vulnerability is understood as their limited physical mobility and their cultural patterned behavior (shy, passive and submissive). To make this point clear, Dyal-Chand (2007) cited an example from a GB branch where a woman failed to pay installments for a few weeks and was brought to the bank office by her peers. The Bank workers asked the woman to sit inside a room in the bank and locked the door from outside. That woman felt so humiliated that she hanged herself from the roof fan by using her own *sari* (women's clothing in rural Bangladesh).

On April 14, 2010, a television program in Bangladesh aired a surprising incident. A few youths in a village in northern Bangladesh took their own lives after failing to repay their loans. The tragedies were attributed to exorbitant interest rates, which trapped the borrowers into a never-ending debt cycle (Ferdous & Uddin, 2010). In a different incident that took place in Rangpur, a district of northern Bangladesh, poor villagers had been suffering from the extortions of three different groups of people: the corrupt police forces, the greedy and dishonest medical doctors and finally the MFIs (Ashraf, 2011b). In sum, these incidents eventually form a kind of negative impression about the microfinance programs as a whole and consequently reduced participation.

3.6.6. Insufficient Resources

According to Bandura (1982), the concept of perceived control or self-efficacy is equivalent to the likelihood of behavioral performance based on capital and other endowment available to an individual. Perceived control beliefs are the beliefs that include both internal and external variables which might ease or hinder the achievement of intended behavior. External factors include environmental factors such as beliefs about sufficiency of resources and opportunities (Noble, 2010). Together, these factors will determine the intention toward participatory behavior, based on an adequate level of the individual's effective control over the intended behavior (Kriek & Stols, 2010). In their study, Fen and Hong (2009) found that time and money affected individual participation in exercise practice among young men.

Zaman (2004) noted that the poorest of Bangladesh have a number of constraints such as fewer income sources, poor health and poor education. Because the poor villagers do not have insufficient resources, MFIs management generally feel that they are at risk from paying back their loan. In the rural areas of Bangladesh, insufficiency of resources of the rural poor was frequently observed as an important impediment of participation in MFIs (Lee, 2009; Montgomery, 1996). Montgomery (1996) used case studies to explore the disadvantages of group lending of MFIs in Bangladesh. He suggested that the microcredit programs should meet the need of the poor borrowers. This could be done through flexible repayment scheduling, savings facilities and short-term consumption loans. In this way, he opined, the poor could be rescued from socially damaging peer pressure lending practices.

Time along with its allocation (how much time to spend on different tasks) is also considered to be another important resource which may constraint some individuals to participate (Dewhurst, Hancock & Ellsworth, 2013). This element is particularly applicable to the rural women for whom time has an opportunity cost which may not be affordable by them (Evans et al., 1999; Noble, 2010). With respect to how time was a constraint to women, Rahman (1999) described a case where women had to bear the consequences in juggling between family and MFI participation. In one instance, the wife got beaten by her husband because she could not reach home on time to prepare his morning meal as a result of some administrative delays in MFIs. In this case, the husband borrowed money from one of his friends in the neighboring village to pay for loan installment. The husband instructed his wife to pay give the money to the bank worker and to return home after that to prepare his morning meal. The wife, however, was delayed in the center because one member who belonged to her group who was from a distant village did not show up in the meeting. In the loan center, the wife tried to explain her urgency to other members and asked permission from the bank worker to return home. The bank worker refused to accept her installment and did not allow her to leave the loan center until the installment problem was resolved. The woman along with all other members was forced to sit a couple of extra hours in the center before she could return home. The husband was furious toward his wife for returning home late and refused to accept any explanation about her delay in the center. As a result, she was beaten by her husband. This case shows how time can be an important element for women in juggling between a family life and participation in MFIs. Lee (2009) also noted that some microcredit programs lack flexibility because the MFIs have short opening hours during weekdays.

Duong and Izumida (2002) examined the microfinance programs in Vietnam. This study used cross-sectional survey conducted in three provinces. The research investigated three dimensions of microcredit programs namely participation of the rural households in the Vietnamese rural credit market, lender behavior in response to the credit needs of rural households and impact of credit. While the formal sector used to lend for the production purposes, the informal sector was diverse. However, the results demonstrated that the poor had difficulties in accessing credit facilities. Without much access to credit facilities, participation was reduced. In this context, access represented a form of control an individual has over his/her behavior.

Meyer (2002) reviewed the microfinance industry in Bangladesh along with its contemporary constraints which include high dropout rates, exclusion and non-participation, evidence of unmet demand, delinquencies and defaults, overlap, inflexible product characteristics and product design, etc. Based on qualitative analysis of the previous surveys and case studies, he noted a huge expansion of microfinance in Bangladesh which has led to intense competition for clients that may undermine the industry.

3.6.7. Lack of Business Knowledge

Lack of knowledge is considered in TPB as one of the potential barriers of self-efficacy (Ajzen, 1985). Knowledge is like a fluid mix of framed experience, values, contextual information and expert insights (Glass, 2001). Paulo Freire's subaltern philosophy asserts that knowledge is constructed by forming and testing empirical hypotheses intended to reestablish smooth functioning or enlarge effective coping habits (Glass, 2001). Sharing of knowledge refers to reciprocal exchange of ideas on a joint collaboration (van den Hooff & de Ridder, 2004), which indicates teamwork and cooperation of every group member devoted to achieve a common goal. It is sometimes assumed that sharing of knowledge resembles other deliberate behavioral conducts, such as pro-social behaviors and organizational citizenship behaviors.

Across a broad range of literatures, a consensus has emerged that our society is moving toward postindustrial or post-bureaucratic society in which knowledge and information is argued to enhance economic growth (Benkler, 2006; Castells, 2000; Drewharst et al., 2013; Huber, 2004; Powell & Snellman, 2004; Teece, 2003). Studies have shown that lack of information and knowledge tends to hinder people from making decisions. As Noble (2010) found, lack of knowledge or program awareness or widespread misinformation was the reason some people did not participate in any particular activity. He further noted that some nonparticipants reported that they knew about the program but lack specific information about availability, eligibility requirements and procedures for application. Accurate program information with formal outreach, referral mechanisms, word-of mouth and personal program experience were found to be important for program participation (Lee, 2009). According to Huber (2004), there has been a disability of knowledge of potential clients that compromises their understanding of the benefits of credit. As a result, Huber concluded that the level of poverty was often double among the illiterates and the figure had been nearly tripled in the case of extreme poverty incidence.

Ferdous and Udding (2010) unleashed a grim fact of misinformation and ignorance about microcredit. They reported that the way the field officers of MFIs marketed the loans was like sales executives of commercial banks marketed personal loans and credit cards. As a result, the poor tended to perceive that the main objective of the field officers of MFIs was to sell loans, not to change lives. It saddled the loan recipients with the insidious burden of dependency contrary to economic freedom. In addition to this reality, they cited one villager as saying the following:

> "In the beginning, the NGOs told us their loans would bring joy to our lives if we borrowed from them and started a business. They lured us into the loans by telling that we would have chickens, latrines, and many

> other things to lead a good life. That good life became obvious as we sank deeper into the quicksand of illusion created by them. This illusion eventually tightens around our neck like a noose" (pp. 43).

Mosley and Rock (2004) examined qualitatively six MFIs in Africa and assessed their level of participation and impact on poverty. The impact of microfinance was found to vary between institutions, especially in South Africa and Kenya. They, however, recognized that microfinance, irrespective of their proximate recipient (i.e., whether they were poor or not), improved human capital via augmented spending on education and related improvements in health, which could have intra-household and intergenerational effects.

3.6.8. Poor Health or Vulnerability to Crisis

In a TPB model, Ajzen (1991) advocated that a person's perceived behavioral control varies across situations. Within the TPB framework, the PBC construct is synonymous with self-efficacy. Casper (2007) opined that inability due to illness and lack of opportunity are the factors that could hinder individual control toward intention and participation in certain activities. According to Noble (2010), there was ample evidence that poor health or vulnerability to crisis appeared to be potential participation barrier.

Vulnerability is an important concern in the case of poor section of the population in society. It can be characterized by the risk of getting into deeper poverty due to several reasons. The extent of vulnerability in Bangladesh is very large. A high density of spending on consumption expenditure indicates that it can have big shocks on the rate of poverty change. The relative status of poverty lines and their probability density function implies that even a tiny shock can push a considerable number of the poor into extreme suffering and deprivation (Ahmed, Narayan, & Zaman, 2009). Similar type of social vulnerability is also common in the society of many provinces in India (Roodman, 2013).

Rahman (1999) found that natural disaster due to irregular contingencies could have a devastating impact on the poverty dynamics in Bangladesh. Zaman (2004) asserted that asset creation through capital accumulation was paramount to reduce household vulnerability of the rural poor households. In this way, MFIs might serve as an important tool to trim down the vulnerability by providing emergency assistance in situations of severe cataclysm, such as the recent floods in Bangladesh. As a matter of fact, MFIs turned into *de facto* relief to organizations and played an essential role in sustaining the socioeconomic status of the people in the wake of a natural disaster. Indeed, these types of financial and social aids to the poor after the disaster were deemed to be highly valued by microfinance participants.

Amin, Rai, and Topa (2003) evaluated outreach of the GB in the cases of the extreme poor and vulnerable in two villages in Bangladesh. The study used a unique panel data comprising monthly consumption and income collected from 229 households of those two villages. The results suggested that the performance of the program was at a satisfactory level in terms of reaching the poor but the group of vulnerable poor was still beyond reach. This finding implied that participation of the vulnerable poor in microfinance program was still in an unsatisfactory level which warrants further attention in order to alleviate rural hard core poverty in Bangladesh.

Mosley and Rock (2004) dealt with the household risk management capacity of the poor microfinance recipients. They reported that the households risk management capacity of the poor could be developed through deliberate training and capacity-building sessions. They also urged that microfinance programs should allow part of the loan proceeds into the formation of social networks. However, this might create ‘poverty externalities’ for extending the group of credit recipients to include more poor people. Yet, the positive consequence was that it would create stabilization of village income which could diminish the vulnerability of the poorest to risk.

Walker and Matin (2006) attempted to find out the way social, financial and human foundations could be built up for the Specially

Targeted Ultra-Poor (STUP). The principal idea behind this mechanism was to cater to the STUP with an integrated back-up program in a comprehensive manner for the period of 18 months. The study expected that after this period of time the ultra-poor segment of society could take part in development-oriented programs and could ensure good uses of services provided by MFIs. The study tried to discern the participation patterns of the rural poor by incorporating several factors that could change the level of participation. The study collected case stories to discover unique trends in the changes of perceptions of the STUP participants after participating in the program. Opinions of the majority of the participants revealed that there was a positive change in their capability to tackle potential economic shocks. The different capabilities were then ranked. Participants were ranked first when they were able to: (a) increase or improve their non-land and land assets the most; (b) manage to secure three meals a day; (c) own their homestead land; and (d) engage in additional income-earning activities, or diversify into other profitable forms for income generation. Participants were ranked the last (i.e., Rank 4) when they did not own land assets, do not work too much beyond their STUP assets, and have substantial spending on health issues.

The findings of the study suggested that more than 80 percent of the change happened to the group who owned homestead and that had a household head who was physically able. About 45 percent change occurred in the group who did not own homestead and had a household head who was physically able. Forty percent change took place in the group who owned homestead and had a household head who was physically not able. And 20 percent change took place for the group who did not own homestead.

CARE[5] Bangladesh (2005) was much concerned about the vulnerability of the poor in Bangladesh. According to its view the ultra-poor and poor people were substantially vulnerable and they had very limited capabilities to handle risk. In order to minimize risk, the poor

[5] Cooperative for American Relief Everywhere has been working in Bangladesh since the liberation period.

people often took different measures that might push them into a vicious circle of poverty. The study asserted that managing risk measurement was in reality a social or public mechanism rather than an individual or private matter. Household-related risks were related with several independent factors which linked many other socioeconomic parameters such as economic development, poverty reduction, social cohesion and environmental aspect. Thus, a holistic approach to risk management, or "social risk management" is essential. In fact, a wider space of joint private and public efforts could ensure good management of risk in a vulnerable environment. Social risk management approach could be initiated with an asset-based approach that could offer an integrated mechanism encompassing household, community and extra-community assets and risk management strategies. This is because in the wake of a vulnerability crisis, the rural poor tend to face problem in getting membership in MFIs.

CGAP[6] report (2001) maintained that microfinance programs have an effective impact on targeting and reaching the poor, but many other reports indicated that the poorest were deliberately ignored and hence excluded. The main reason behind this was that most of the prominent MFIs paid less attention in selecting more vulnerable clients. Very often, the poorest also remained self-excluded. However, there were, according to this report, a few programs which had effectively reached the poorest. One of such programs was the Income Generation for Vulnerable Groups Development (IGVGD) Program operated by BRAC, the largest NGO-MFI in Bangladesh. The main objective of the IGVGD Program was to provide financial supports by extending microloans to the most destitute poor based on governmental food security intervention. This joint collaboration over the last ten years between the government and BRAC had become successful in the delivery of food grain assistance and savings and credit services to nearly a million women in Bangladesh.

---

[6] The Consultative Group to Assist the Poor is a global partnership of leading organizations that seek to increase access to the financial services the poor need to improve their lives.

3.7. Chapter Summary

This chapter presented the theoretical background and a critical review of literature on participation and nonparticipation of the rural poor in MFIs in Bangladesh as well as in a global perspective. The study incorporated TPB as its theoretical background which consists of intention as an antecedent of actual behavior. Three independent variables such as attitude, subjective norms and perceived behavioral control were also considered in influencing intention toward actual behavior. The study also included the rationale for the adoption of the TPB model in explaining participation and nonparticipation of the rural poor in MFIs.

In the literature review, it first discussed the theory and its constructs of the TPB model. Then, it presented a critical review of extensive literature on eight external factors that are purported to influence participation and nonparticipation of the rural poor in MFIs in Bangladesh and in other countries of the world. The discussion in this chapter showed that the TPB framework was rarely applied in the context of nonparticipation and participation in MFIs. It also reviewed the literature to put arguments on why the factors were included to explain participatory as well as non-participatory behaviors of the rural poor in MFIs in Bangladesh.

Chapter 4

METHODOLOGY

4.1. INTRODUCTION

The general objective of this treatise is to gain an understanding of the factors that influence the rural poor's decision to participate or not to participate in their local MFIs in Bangladesh. To achieve this intended objective, TPB was used as the theoretical framework for this study. In this study, a set of explanatory variables (or factors) was included to determine if they add predictive value to the model. These variables are fear of risk associated with loans, individual preference on nonparticipation, religious leaders' lecture on nonparticipation, spousal dislike of female heading the household, friends' advice, and insufficiency of resources, lack of knowledge and poor health or vulnerability to crisis.

This chapter begins with a conceptual approach and methodology used in the study. This is followed by a critical evaluation of the TPB model in terms of nonparticipation of the rural poor in MFIs in Bangladesh. Thus, the study was intended to examine the factors of nonparticipation using the TPB framework. In so doing, the study used a closed-ended questionnaire to collect the relevant data.

The present study had five specific objectives. To attain these objectives, logistic regression and ordinary multiple regression analyses were performed because of the binary nature of the dependent variable.

4.2. RESEARCH MODELS

This study was a basic or fundamental research. The main purpose of this study was to validate the applicability of the TPB model in explaining the phenomenon on nonparticipation of the rural poor in MFIs in Bangladesh (Sommer, 2011). There are three independent variables in the TPB model. They are attitude, subjective norm, and PBC, which are purported to influence intention toward specific behavior.

The study added eight new external variables as the immediate antecedents of attitude, subjective norms and PBC, which consequently influence intention toward nonparticipation. Among eight variables, attitude has two antecedents (Fear of risk associated with loans and individual preference), subjective norms have three (religious leaders lectures, spousal dislike of female head of household and friends' negative advice) and PBC has three (insufficiency of resources, lack of business knowledge and poor health or vulnerability to crises). If some variance in microfinance nonparticipation by the rural poor can be explained by adding external variables, then the use of TPB can be applied in future studies. The theory may also help understand the potential barriers of participation in MFIs. The following were the research models to be tested, developed based on the TPB framework.

Model 1:

$Y = f\,(X_1\ X_2,\ X_{3,},\ X_4,\ X_5,\ X_6,\ X_7,\ X_8,\ X_9,\ X_{10},\ X_{11},\ X_{12},\ X_{13},\ X_{15},\ X_{16},\ X_{17},\ X_{18},\ X_{19})$

Where,

Y = Nonparticipation (Yes = 1, No = 0)

X_1 = Gender

X_2 = Age
X_3 = Marital Status
X_4 = Education
X_5 = Yearly income
X_6 = Total amount of land
X_7 = Assets other than land
X_8 = Intention
X_9 = Attitude
X_{10} = Subjective norms (SN)
X_{11} = Perceived behavioral control (PBC)
X_{12} = Fear of risk associated with loans
X_{13} = Individual preferences
X_{14} = Religious leaders' lecture
X_{15} = Spousal dislike of female heading the household
X_{16} = Friends' advice
X_{17} = Insufficient resources
X_{18} = Lack of knowledge
X_{19} = Poor health or vulnerability to crises

Model 2:

$Y = f (X_1\ X_2, X_{3,}, X_4, X_5, X_6, X_7, X_8)$

Where,

Y = Nonparticipation (Yes = 1, No = 0)
X_1 = Fear of risk associated with loan
X_2 = Individual preference
X_3 = Religious leaders lectures
X_4 = Spousal dislike of female heading the household
X_5 = Friends' negative advice
X_6 = Insufficient resources
X_7 = Lack of knowledge
X_8 = Poor health or vulnerability to crises

Model 3:

$Y = f(X_1, X_2, X_3)$

Where,

Y = Intention

X_1 = Attitude

X_2 = Subjective norms (SN)

X_3 = Perceived behavioral control (PBC)

Model 4:

$Y = f(X_1, X_2)$

Where,

Y = Attitude

X_1 = Fear of risk associated with loans

X_2 = Individual preference

Model 5:

$Y = f(X_1, X_2, X_3)$

Where,

Y = SN

X_1 = Religious instructions

X_2 = Spousal dislike of female heading the household

X_3 = Friends' negative advice

Model 6:

$Y = f(X_1, X_2, X_3)$

Where,

Y = PBC

X_1 = Resource insufficiency

X_2 = Lack of business knowledge

X_3 = Poor health or vulnerability to crises

As mentioned earlier, a survey design methodology is employed in this study. This particular design is useful because both attitudes and behaviors are tested (Sommer, 2011), using samples drawn from six different districts of Bangladesh. This study is cross-sectional since the surveys have been done at one point in time.

4.3. Hypotheses/Propositions Development

The research models used in the study hinged on the TPB model. The actual behavior in question was nonparticipation of the rural poor in MFIs. In the TPB model intention is postulated as an important determinant of actual behavior. So attitudes, subjective norms, perceived behavioral control and participation or nonparticipation are purported to be indirectly linked through the intention variable. So based on these relationships, five hypotheses were developed as H_1, H_2, H_3, H_4 and H_5.

Hypotheses 6, 7, 8, 9, 10, 11, 12, and 13 were proposed by incorporating fear of risk, individual preferences, religious leaders' lectures, spousal dislike, friends' advice, insufficient resources, lack of knowledge, and poor health or vulnerability to crisis. These variables were postulated as the antecedents of participation or nonparticipation of the rural poor in the MFIs. Thus, all 13 hypotheses developed are as follows:

4.3.1. Intention

Intention was posited as the antecedent of actual behavior in the TPB model (Ajzen & Fishbein, 2000). They argued that an individual is likely to perform an actual behavior when he/she has the intention to do so. In the context of the study, behavioral intention referred to the rural poor's experience in microfinance programs, while participation (or nonparticipation) was the actual behavior.

There is extensive evidence in the social psychological literature (e.g., Ajzen, 1991) supporting the role of intention as a predictor of behavior across a wide variety of domains. Meta-analysis of more than 80 studies observed an average intention behavior correlation. According to Ajzen and Fishbein (1980), intention is the immediate determinant of behavior and when an appropriate measure of intention is obtained at the same level of specification as the behavior, it will provide the most accurate prediction of behavior. Thus, it was hypothesized as:

> *H_1 Intention is positively related with the nonparticipation of the rural poor in MFIs.*

4.3.2. Attitudes

Among the three antecedents, attitude toward behavioral intention has been investigated in many studies in various fields, such as, Galani-Moutafi (2000) in anthropology and Stedman (2002) in social psychology. Generally, attitude focuses on individual preference on choosing a particular behavioral action. Ajzen and Fishbein (1980) traced the origin of using attitude in social behavioral studies. They found that various studies had investigated attitudes in terms of their conceptualization. However, Fishbein and Ajzen (1975) asserted that even though attitudes could not explain a behavior exclusively, it could explain the behavior much accurately than any other single variable (Lee, 2011).

Ajzen (1991) defined attitude as "to the degree to which a person has a favorable or unfavorable evaluation or appraisal of the behavior in question" (p.188). Attitudinal behavior of an individual person focuses on the ultimate consequences of the behavior and her/his overall assessment of the pertinent outcome. In fact, attitude toward a behavior can lead to the formation of a behavioral intention (Ajzen, 1991).

Studies tended to find a causal relationship between attitudes and behavior (Anker, Freely, & Kim, 2010; Kaiser & Schultz, 2009; Mason & Cheyne, 2000; Smith et al. 2008; Suhayati, 2012). However, the attitude-behavior relation tended to be weak. According to Fishbein and Ajzen

(1975), attitude may influence behavior indirectly through the variable of intention. Indeed, evidence showed a positive relationship between attitude and intention to behave (Bergkvist, 2009; Okun & Sloane, 2002). Hence, it was hypothesized that:

> H_2 *Attitude is positively related to intention toward participation (or nonparticipation) of the rural poor in MFIs.*

4.3.3. Subjective Norms

Subjective norms are contingent on normative beliefs and motivation reinforced by the pressure of people who are important to the individual person in performing a particular behavior. According to Ajzen (1991, p. 188), subjective norm is "the perceived social pressure to perform or not to perform the behavior." It is argued that the individual is likely to comply with the wishes of the referent others if they are important to him/her (Fu, Hughes, Richards, Hughes & Jones, 2010; Manning, 2011). Subjective perception of an individual about the normative surrounding together with attitude can predict intention (Fishbein & Ajzen, 1975), as postulated by TPB. This fact implies that an individual complies with the influence from some others who are important or influential in the society (Venkatesh & Davis, 2000).

In the case of participation of the rural poor in MFIs, some influential personalities can be of important dynamics in motivating the rural poor to participate or not to participate in microfinance programs. In this regard, family friends, spouse, relatives, and religious leaders can have strong influence on the formation of intention of an individual (Armitage & Christian, 2003). Similarly, friends could be an influential referral to influence participation (or nonparticipation) in any certain activity (Beadnell et al., 2007). Hence, the following was hypothesized:

> H_3 *Subjective norms are positively related with intention toward nonparticipation of the rural poor in MFIs.*

4.3.4. Perceived Behavioral Control (PBC)

According to Ajzen (1991), the importance of control on actual behavior is self-evident. Any behavioral achievement must depend upon the availability of required resources and relevant opportunities. That is, if an individual does not have complete control over the activity, it may never take place. Control may be in the form of adequate resources or time, which is the precondition to perform that specific behavior. In this regard, PBC plays an important role in TPB. Evans et al. (1999) demonstrated that many people in the rural areas of Bangladesh did not participate in microfinance programs because they did not possess the necessary resources and time to do so. Thus,

> H_4 *PBC is positively related with intention toward nonparticipation of the rural poor in MFIs.*

4.3.5. Direct Effects of PBC on Nonparticipation

According to Ajzen (1991), PBC can be directly linked to behavioral achievement for two reasons. Firstly, when a person perceives that there is a lack of volitional control, he/she will not perform that behavior. Secondly, PBC is often utilized as a substitute for a measure of actual control. This is because when the availability of resources and opportunities is perceived to be realistic, the probability of a successful behavioral achievement is high (Ajzen, 1985, 1991; Armitage & Christian, 2003). Hence, it was proposed that:

> H_5 *PBC is directly and positively related with the nonparticipation of the rural poor in MFIs.*

4.3.6. Selected Factors Affecting Nonparticipation of the Rural Poor in MFIs

In addition to the three determinants of behavioral intention, this study considered other factors postulated to affect nonparticipation of the rural poor in MFIs. These factors are elaborated next.

4.3.7. Fear of Risks Associated with Loans

Some individuals are risk averse due to experienced fear. According to Lockwood (2011), for many, fear is triggered when they consider the negative outcomes they could experience as a result of entering risky situations. Thus, fear is associated with a risk factor which ought to be considered in explaining nonparticipation of the rural poor in MFIs.

The term 'risk' is believed to be originated in the Middle Ages and was related to maritime insurance to the difficulties one could face at sea (Breivik, 2007). In contemporary times, the usage of the term 'risk' is rooted in early economic theory, where risk is defined in utility theory and therefore relates to the estimate of the likelihood and magnitude of potential costs and benefits. However, more recent approaches to the study of risk acknowledge the limitations to this approach and almost exclusively focus on the perceptions of loss, cost, harm or other terms used to denote the negative consequences (Breivik, 2007). However, within the context of this study, the extensive debates concerning the issue stated above are not the primary focus. What matters in this study is the risk in relation to the people's motivations for microfinance participation (Mukherji & Wright, 2002). In this context, risk is interpreted as one or both of: (a) the judgments of uncertainty that people make about any potential harmful outcomes of their participation; and (b) those potentially harmful outcomes.

In behavioral theory, a number of contextual variables are integral to the decision-making process. These contextual variables include aspirations and expectations as well as income stream variability or risk

(Mukherji & Wright, 2002). Fear of risk associated with loans stems from several incidents that happened in rural Bangladesh. Rahman (1999) cited several examples where workers of the NGO-MFIs used to detain the village women borrowers and members if they missed to pay the weekly installments. In some extreme cases, the workers of the NGO-MFIs seized the household assets of the poor borrowers including the wooden pillars and tin-roof of the houses for missing the installment of the loans. Rahman (1999) also mentioned that many rural poor members of the NGO-MFIs used to pay the installment of the loans by borrowing from other formal and informal sources. This created a vicious circle of overlapping loans and worse economic outcome. All these instances can shape the rural poor's attitudes negatively toward participation in MFIs in Bangladesh. Thus, it was hypothesized that:

> H_6 *Fear of risk associated with loan is negatively related to the attitude of the rural poor toward intended nonparticipation in MFIs.*

4.3.8. Individual Preferences and Intended Nonparticipation

Individual preferences may affect the attitudes toward nonparticipation and attitudes account for significantly more of the variance in individuals' desires or preferences than intention or self-prediction (Armitage & Conner, 2001). Ajzen (2007) referred to personal desirability or preferences toward a behavior as the degree to which performance of the behavior is positively or negatively valued. According to Jackson (1988, 2005), individual preferences were found to inhibit participation. External constraints act as a barrier to actual participation. Past research has indicated that negative signals or threatening events negativity affected an adaptive function (Ajzen, 2007). These adaptive actions include ways to avoid, escape, or overcome the threatening events, and efforts made to change the routines and the set of decision rules. These action preferences would be associated with negative signals regarding low organizational resources and inferior performance, as well as the negative framing of problems (Mukherji & Wright, 2002). Thus, individual preferences could affect the nonparticipation behaviors of the rural poor in MFIs.

The original Grameen approach was to lend to individual borrowers in the village by forming loan groups. In this program, the individual was kept in line by a considerable amount of pressure from the other members of the group. The group and the loan center in this system functioned as institutions to ensure mutual accountability. The peer pressure, along with the institutional and moral coercion that bank workers in the village exercised on women borrowers, helped the local branch of the MFIs to achieve and maintain a 98 percent repayment rate (Mukherji & Wright, 2002). However, such peer-pressure and institutional coercion on women in the study village also produced unintended consequences for the borrowers and their households (Rahman, 1999). This particular object of unintended outcomes led the rural women to form an individual preference which influenced attitudes toward nonparticipation of the rural poor in MFIs. Thus, it was hypothesized that:

> H_7 *Individual preferences are negatively related with the attitude of the rural poor toward intended nonparticipation in MFIs.*

4.3.9. Religious Leaders' Lecture

Religion is a system of beliefs and practices by which a group of people interprets and responds to what they feel is sacred (Kahf, 2004). Most religion prescribes or prohibits certain behavior in economic, financial and entrepreneurial realms. Kahf (2004) also asserted that different religious groups are likely to make business decisions which are influenced by their religious identity and instructions. Such a phenomenon is widely acknowledged in international business and marketing concepts.

Bidin (2008) explored *zakat* compliance behavior among Muslim employees using theory of planned behavior. He incorporated a religious value index as a predictor of intention to pay *zakat*. He found that Islamic principles had a significant relationship with nonparticipation.

In Islam, interest is strictly forbidden. Using this principle, religious leaders have been discouraging people from participating in any interest-based financial activity. Besides, Islam also prescribes how Muslim women should dress and behave in public places. Hence, it was postulated that:

H_8 *Religious leaders' lectures are negatively related to the subjective norms of the rural poor toward intended nonparticipation in MFIs.*

4.3.10. Spousal Dislike of Female Heading the Households and Intended Nonparticipation

TPB postulates subjective norm as a social factor which refers to social pressure to perform or not to perform the actual behavior (Ajzen, 1991). Subjective norm is considered to be a function of salient normative beliefs. While subjective norm relates to perceptions of *general* social pressure, the underlying normative beliefs are concerned with the likelihood that specific individuals or groups (referents) with whom the individual is motivated to comply will approve or disapprove of the behavior (Armitage & Conner, 2001). Spouse is considered one of the important social referents in the TPB framework (Ajzen, 1985). Hence, the following hypothesis was offered:

H_9 *Spousal dislike of female heading the household is negatively related with the subjective norms of the rural poor toward intended nonparticipation in MFIs.*

4.3.11. Friends' Advice and Intended Nonparticipation

Another important referent is friends who advise others whether to be or not to be involved in specific activities (Ajzen, 1985). White and Wellington (2009) used TPB to predict intentions to participate in group parenting education. Their analyses supported the TPB predictors of participation intentions with self-identity and group norm. Their findings provided preliminary support for social influence and among the sources of social influence, friends were found to be a significant referent that prevented individuals from participating in the parenting education programs.

As in the case of microfinance participation, friends are seen as an important social influence to the rural poor in Bangladesh because of various negative incidents that involved women, as narrated earlier. These incidents later spread in the community of the rural areas, which shaped how the people perceived the microfinance programs as a whole. Based on these past experiences, many close relatives and friends may advice the rural poor not to participate in the MFIs. Hence, it was reasonable to hypothesize that:

H_{10} Friends' advice is negatively related with the subjective norms of the rural poor toward intended nonparticipation in MFIs.

4.3.12. Insufficient Resources and Intended Nonparticipation

Resources and opportunities available to an individual are likely to enable an individual to engage in an activity, which are very similar to the concepts of perceived control or self-efficacy (Bandura, 1982). Control beliefs include beliefs about both internal and external factors that may facilitate or impede performance of behavior. External factors include environmental factors such as beliefs about the sufficiency of resources and opportunities infrastructure, support staff and access to computers (Noble, 2010). Together, these factors will determine the intention toward participatory behavior, given a sufficient degree of the individual's actual control over the behavior (Gagne, 2009; Kriek & Stols, 2010).

In their study, Fen and Hong (2009) found that time and money affected individual nonparticipation. Lee (2009) argued that insufficient resources are reasons for nonparticipation which can be characterized in three ways: (a) perception of need, (b) program features, and (c) program awareness. Some individuals may be reluctant to participate in any charitable program because of their pride, whereas some low-income individuals participate in food assistance program because of economic imperatives. Another obstacle for participation is the lack of program flexibility (Lee, 2009). When program centers open only in certain hours of the day, participation is limited. As mentioned earlier by Rahman (1999), balancing between work and family brought about by participation in MFIs was a struggle for many women. Because women are expected to cater for their family most of the time, lack of such important resource (i.e., time) may limit their participation in MFIs. Hence, it was hypothesized that:

H_{11} Insufficient resources are negatively related to PBC of the rural poor toward intended nonparticipation in MFIs.

4.3.13. Lack of Entrepreneurial/Business Knowledge and Intended Nonparticipation

Lack of knowledge is one of the potential barriers of self-efficacy (Ajzen, 1985). Knowledge is like a fluid mix of framed experience, values, contextual information and expert insights (Glass, 2001). Knowledge has utility when it is used, which suggests that it needs to be shared. Knowledge sharing is the process of mutually exchanging knowledge and jointly creating new knowledge (van den Hooff & de Ridder, 2004), which implies synergistic collaboration of individuals who work toward a common goal. It is often assumed that knowledge sharing behavior shares similarities with many other voluntary behaviors, such as, helping and pro-social behaviors and organizational citizenship behaviors.

Lack of entrepreneurial knowledge has been argued to be a reason for nonparticipation in any activity (Noble, 2010). Some nonparticipants revealed that they knew about the program but lack specific information about the availability, eligibility requirements and procedures for proper use of the loans. Accurate program information with formal outreach, referral mechanisms, word-of mouth and personal program experience are important to program participation (Lee, 2009). Hence, it was hypothesized that:

H_{12} Lack of knowledge of the rural poor is negatively related with PBC toward intended nonparticipation in MFIs.

4.3.14. Poor Health or Vulnerability to Crisis and Intended Nonparticipation

Ajzen (1991) advocated that a person's PBC may vary across situations and actions. Within the TPB framework, the PBC construct is synonymous with self-efficacy. Casper (2007) opined that poor health and lack of opportunity are some of factors that can hinder perceived behavioral control toward intention and nonparticipation in certain activities. According to Noble (2010), there is ample evidence that poor health or vulnerability to crisis were reasons for nonparticipation of the rural poor in MFIs. Thus, the following hypothesis was proposed:

H_{13} Poor health or vulnerability to crisis is negatively related with PBC of the rural poor toward intended nonparticipation in MFIs.

4.4. Research Design

This section discusses the methods and techniques applied to conduct the study. This study was a field survey, conducted in a non-contrived setting, and with no interference in the normal flow of events. The data collection exercises were aimed at gathering information in identifying the factors affecting participation and nonparticipation of the households who are poor but are eligible to take part in microcredit programs. As there were rural poor who participated and did not participate in MFIs, the study collected data from these two groups of people in six major districts of Bangladesh. Data were analyzed at the individual level. Figure 4.1 illustrates the flow of the research design.

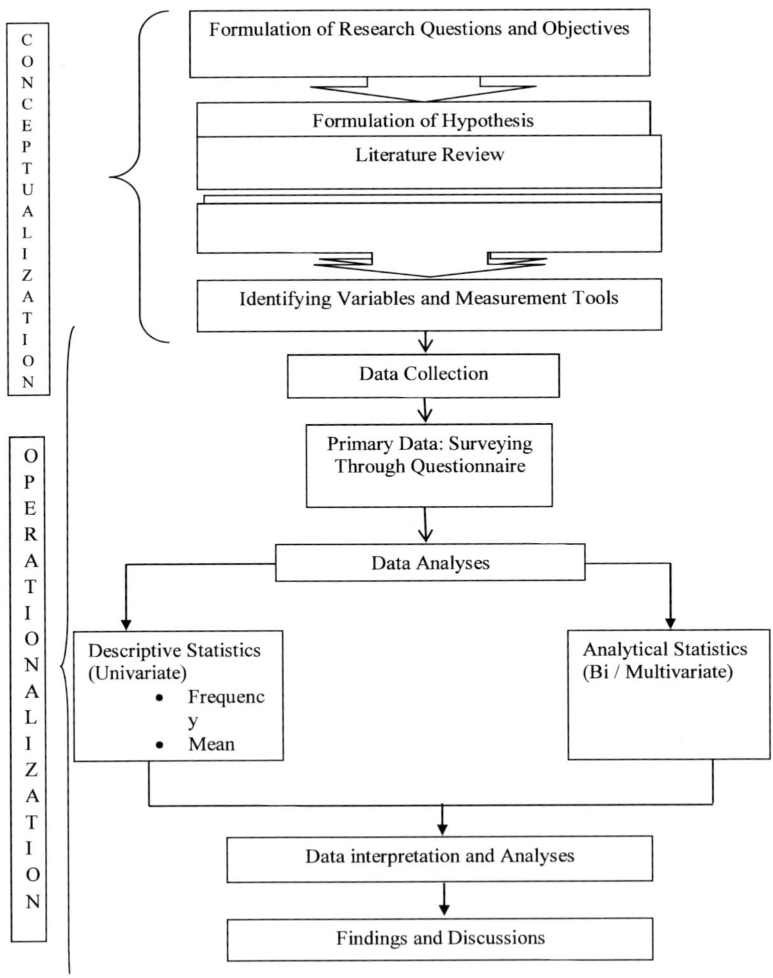

Figure 4.1. Research design for the study.

4.5. MEASUREMENT OF VARIABLES

This section discusses measurement of the variables. A five point-Likert scale (Weijters, Cabooter, & Schillewaert, 2010) was primarily used to measure the variables. In addition, an open-ended question was asked to allow the respondents to provide any additional information on microfinance participation. The feedback of this type of information has been incorporated in the research findings of the study. The study also collected additional information regarding the perception of the rural poor about the overall experience gathered from the borrowing microfinance from MFIs.

4.5.1. Dependent Variables

Nonparticipation

The dependent variable for this study is the actual behavior of nonparticipation or participation in the MFIs. There is a debate about how the variable should be measured (Jang, Bai, Hu & Wu, 2009). For measuring nonparticipation or participation variable, the present study used single dichotomous (yes or no) question item, "Are you participating in MFIs now?" following Ashraf (2011c) and George (2004). Though multiple-item scales are preferred in most cases (Jicha, 2011; Naylor, 2011), a single item will suffice in some instances, as when individuals respond to a single item with high degrees of accuracy (Ashraf, 2011c; Flores, 2012; George, 2004). There were also seven demographic questions included in the instrument which is provided in the Appendix.

Intention

The dependent variable for this study is the poor villagers' intended nonparticipation. Intention has been used in this study as an intervening variable. It was found that most of the studies employed more than single item for this construct (Lee, 2002). Like nonparticipation variable, the intention variable can be measured either using a Likert scale (Park and

Lee, 2009) or dichotomy (Jang, Bai, Hu and Wu, 2009). However, items for this variable are based on those used in previous research of Hedzir (2009) which is similar to the present study using five items for measuring intention variable.

4.5.2. Independent Variables

Attitudes

Attitude is measured in the domain of nonparticipation in MFIs using the opinion of the rural poor. As mentioned earlier, the application of TPB framework in microfinance programs is not common. However, in other fields of social psychology, business management, technology adoption, its application is plenty such as, sleep hygiene (von Linden, 2010), online education (Knabe, 2012), employee theft in retailing (Emilus, 2011) and technology adoption (Jackson, Quaddus, Islam & Stanton, 2006). However, the items for the attitude variable for this study was constructed based on Ashraf (2011c) and Zini (2002) which used multiple items under the Likert scale of measurement. The present study followed the studies of Ashraf (2011c) which sought to explore the participation status of the rural poor in MFIs in Bangladesh using TPB as its guiding principle. The study of Zini (2002) is also similar in terms of focusing on the participation status of the labor union members.

Subjective Norms

The next variable, subjective norms, was measured using three referents, such as religious leaders (four items), family members namely, spouse (three items) and friends (four items). For selecting the items for subjective norms within the TPB framework, there are both traditions of using small and large number of items. However, small items could lead to a poor measurement outcome (Armitage & Conner, 2001; Povey et al., 2000; Sun, Guo, Want & Sun, 2006). Each of the items was measured using a five point-Likert scale, ranging from 1 being Strongly Disagree to 5 being Strongly Agree. For this study, items of subjective norms were selected based on Ashraf (2011c) which studied the participation of the rural poor in Bangladesh. It had used three items referring religious leaders, spouse and friends.

Perceived Behavioral Control (PBC)

As mentioned earlier, the theory of planned behavior is open to include additional predictors that can be beneficial to explain a specific behavior of action (Ajzen, 1991). The special feature and component of TPB is its perceived behavioral component which differentiates it from TRA with a theoretical robustness for predicting human behavior. Thus, this component of TPB leads researchers to investigate into the level to which an individual's internal and external control variables such as resources, opportunities, skills, ability and barriers are linked with intention toward certain behavioral action (Ajzen, 1988). There have been studies that focused on time, constraints and tight schedules (Sparks, 2007). In the original model, PBC is measured with the items that include perceived competence by which an individual can overpass the obstacle in order to perform certain behaviors (McGehee, 2002).

In the tourism industry, it is common for tourists who intend to travel to foreign lands, they must face various challenges such as foreign culture, unfamiliar language, lack of proper accommodation, exotic food which lead them to overcome all these obstacles that pose as antecedents to potential tourism participation (McGehee & Norman, 2002). However, there are different arguments which demonstrate that PBC beliefs are more correlated with behavioral intention than PBC (Giles et al., 2002; Lemmens, et al. 2005). For this study, PBC is measured in the contexts of insufficiency of resources (4 itmes), lack of knowledge (4 items) and ill-health or vulnerability to crisis (3 items) based on Ashraf (2011c). As mentioned earlier, the study of Ashraf (2011c) was used for the present study because it is similar to the present study exploring the similar object of nonparticipation or participation in MFIs in Bangladesh.

External Variables

One of the attractive features of TPB is that the model can accommodate external factors based on the particular situation in order to augment the predicting power of the model. The present study has chosen eight client-related variables as possible predicting variables toward the poor villagers' intended nonparticipation. There have been several studies which added external variables and found that behavioral performance is augmented (Broad, 2003; Raymond & Hall, 2008; Stoddart & Rogerson, 2004; Wearing, 2001). This study used two external factors as the antecedents of attitude, three factors for subjective norms and three factors for PBC.

Measuring Demographic Variables

Table 4.1. Items used to Measure Each Construct in TPB

Construct	Items
Intention	1. I am eager to participate in the MFIs. 2. I plan not to participate in the MFIs in the future. 3. I intend to participate in the MFIs in the future. 4. I don't expect to participate in the MFIs in the future. 5. I intend to participate in Islamic MFIs.
Attitude	1. I believe that participation in MFIs is a good idea. 2. I believe that participation in MFIs is a bad idea. 3. I believe that participation in Islamic MFIs is a bad idea. 4. I believe that participation in Islamic MFIs is a good idea. 5. I believe that I should participate in MFIs. 6. I believe that I should not participate in MFIs. 7. I consider that the MFIs are good to increase income. 8. I feel that the MFIs are charging a high interest rate. 9. I feel that the risks are high in participating in MFIs. 10. I feel that the MFIs are against the religion of Islam. 11. I feel that women should not be involved in MFIs by violating purdah. 12. I believe that I should not be involved in interest-based MFIs.
Subjective norms	1. My religious leaders inspire me to participate in MFIs. 2. My spouse encourages my participation in MFIs. 3. My friends advise me to participate in MFIs.
Perceived behavioral control	1. I am constrained by insufficient resources. 2. I am constrained by lack of proper knowledge of business. 3. I am constrained by poor health or I am vulnerable to crises.

Similar to other researches, this research included the respondents' basic socio-demographic variables such as gender, age, marital status, education level, amount of asset, land and annual household income. The socio-demographic variables were included in the study in order to better understand the various socio-economic characteristics of the respondents in the sample. These findings are also useful for understanding the respondents' (participants or nonparticipants) eligibility for membership in the MFIs. For this demographic construct, the study consulted the previous studies which are (Lee, 2011; Lockwood, 2011; Sommer, 2011; Cameron, 2010; Ekpe, Mat, & Razak, 2010). Table 4.1 provides a list of items used to measure each construct in the TPB model.

4.6. Data Collection

The data collection exercise was aimed at gathering information on the impact of eight factors that affect participation and nonparticipation of the rural poor in MFIs in Bangladesh through the basic constructs of TPB. To this aim, data were collected by face to face interviews from six selected areas of Bangladesh using closed-end questionnaire. A general objective of survey research is to collect data representative of a population. The researcher used information gathered from the survey to generalize findings from a drawn sample of a population remaining within the limits of random error (Bartlett, Kotrlik & Higgins, 2001).

In order to determine the sample size, the present study uses the procedure suggested by Cochran (1977). According to Cochran (1977), the sample size formula for the categorical data is as follows:

$$n = [(t)^2 * (p)(q)]/(d)^2$$

where,

t = value for selected alpha level of .025 in each tail,

(p)(q) = estimate of variance,

d = acceptable margin of error for proportion being estimated.

Based on this formula, Bartlett et al. (2001) suggested the minimum sample size for the sample population of 1000 is 399. As the total number of participants and nonparticipants (including drop-outs) of the six regions is around 1000 (as it was obtained from the localized MFIs in the regions), the study interviewed 450 individuals in the anticipation that some data might be erroneous or incomplete. Due to errors remained in the data, 420 cases were used for data analysis.

4.6.1. Sampling Procedure

The study areas were selected randomly at two levels. First, six divisions were selected randomly from the total of nine divisions in Bangladesh. Then six districts were selected randomly from six divisions. The districts are Nilphamari, Bogra, Kishoreganj, Maulovibazar, Shariatpur and Satkhira. These six districts were chosen because the people of these regions are poorer and more vulnerable than those in other regions of Bangladesh (Mahmud, 2010). Due to these demographic concerns, the MFIs are operating microfinance programs there (MRA, 2011). These six districts comprised 1,000 individuals of participating and nonparticipating poor in the villages who were predominantly peasants, rickshaw (3-wheel cart) or van pullers and day laborers.

With a view to providing background information for the research, a village profile was created by collecting some benchmark data that included the number of households and population along with socio-economic information. The study covered the areas where the conventional MFIs such as GB, BRAC and ASA are operating which fulfilled the criteria: (i) these villages have microfinance-related activities; (ii) the sampled MFIs have been operating in these locations for at least 15 years; (iii) the poverty characteristics of the places are homogenous in terms of income, household consumption and health situation. These criteria have also been used by previous studies of Hossain (1984, 1985) and Khandker (2006). The exact locations of data collection can be observed in the geopolitical map of Bangladesh (see Figure 4.2).

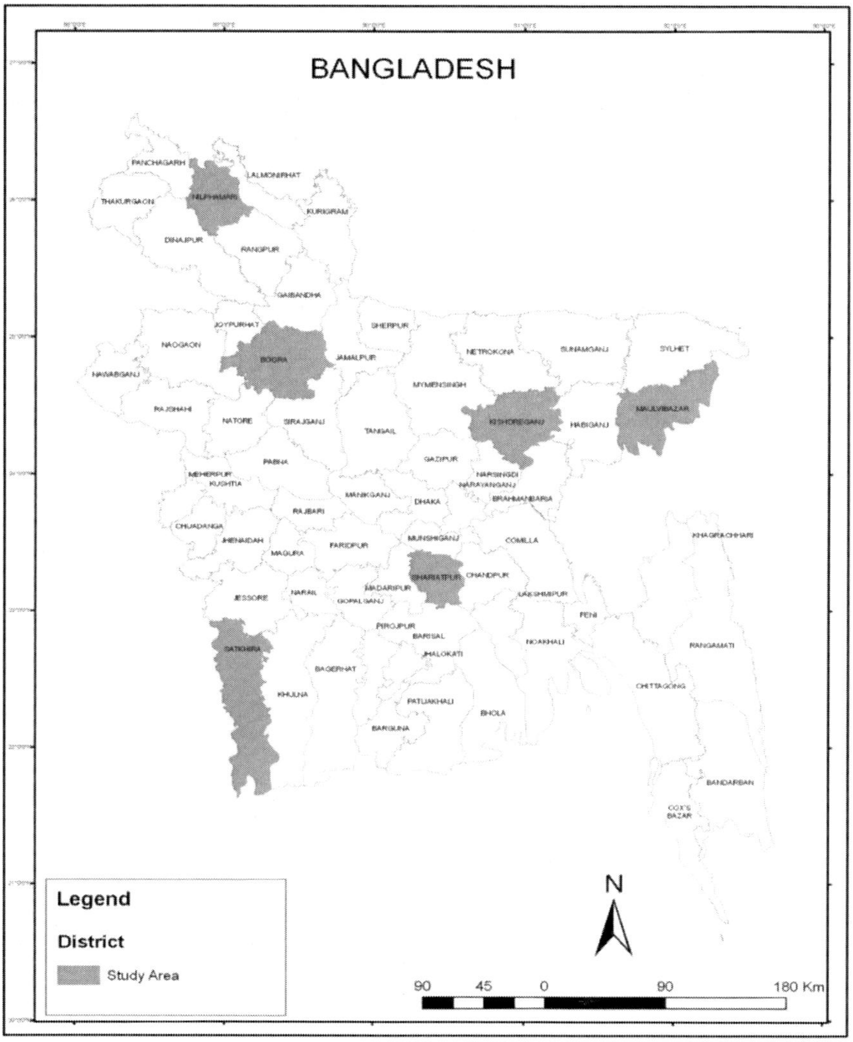

Figure 4.2. Map of Bangladesh showing the study areas.

The samples were drawn based on a random sampling procedure from the list of the rural poor collected from the local offices of the MFIs. The reasons for choosing a simple random sampling were because: (a) this method is applicable when reference population is small, homogenous and readily available; (b) it can increase a sample's statistical efficiency; (c) all subsets of the frame are given an equal probability and each element of the frame thus has an equal probability of selection; (d) it provides for the greatest number of possible samples and this is done by assigning a number to each unit in the sampling frame; and (v) estimates are easy to calculate, and sample can be evenly spread over entire reference population (Anderson, Sweeney, & Williams, 2008).

In the list the participants in the microfinance programs were 410 villagers and more than 600 nonparticipants. These participants and nonparticipants were randomly chosen, but in many cases the target interviewees were not available to be interviewed. According to the villagers, many of the nonparticipants had moved to somewhere else and therefore could not be reached for the interview. Besides, there were some participants who also could not be interviewed because they were temporarily unavailable. Though the study had the target of 75 individuals to interview from each of the six regions, as the population density of these six areas is more or less same (BBS, 2013), these averages cannot be strictly maintained.

4.6.2. Data Collection Procedure

For data collection, ten students, who were most senior and enrolled in the program of Bachelor of Business Administration (BBA) in a private university located in Dhaka, were employed for three months. These students possessed previous experience of similar sorts of data collection for academic purposes and familiarity with the regions selected for surveying. They used to do the similar jobs in their course requirements such as case study analysis and used to collecting primary data from the field.

In addition, a couple of sessions were arranged for their proper training for the face-to-face interview with the mostly illiterate rural village-women. Three sessions of training took place for about six hours in three days. The topics discussed in these sessions were: (a) the possible solutions of practical difficulties faced by the data collectors; (b) how to get temporary shelter in the study areas; (c) how to identify the microfinance participants and nonparticipants; (d) how to meet and approach the village women to provide the information related to microfinance borrowing; and (e) how to conduct interviews with the illiterate women using the closed-end questionnaire. The session also trained about how to avoid misunderstanding on the part of the rural microfinance borrowers who might be suspicious and confused about the right motives of the data collection and how to avoid bias that might arise during data collection.

The author visited every spot of data collection in order to inspect whether the data collection was going on as expected. In this way, the data were checked for possible contamination. The main problems encountered during the data collection phase were: poor communication system from the capital region to the rural spots of data collection and lack of temporary residence and food in the village because of the limited number of hotels and restaurants. The local Union Council Chairman helped the data collectors to have their temporary residence as well as food. Apart from these problems, there had been a prolonged political chaos (national strikes) all over Bangladesh for which data collection was hampered and due to this reason the duration of data collection took three months to complete. On an average, it took an hour to interview an individual respondent. The initial draft of the questionnaire was pilot-tested on a small sample at the outskirt of Dhaka City. A total of 50 cases were obtained. Feedback on the questionnaire was incorporated into the final survey.

4.7. Techniques of Data Analyses

4.7.1. Logistic Regression

Logistic regression was pioneered in the 1940s as an alternative to linear discriminant analysis introduced by Fisher in 1936 in his classification method. It is widely used in many fields, including the medical and social sciences (Schumacker and Lomax, 2011). In economics, it can be used to predict the likelihood of an individual's preference to participate in certain activities. In terms of a business application, it would predict the likelihood of a homeowner defaulting on a mortgage. Conditional random fields are an extension of logistic regression to sequential data which are employed in natural language processing. Following this fact, it is used in this research as in the case of participation or nonparticipation in the programs such as the rural poor's participation or nonparticipation in MFIs.

For attaining the answers of the research questions of this study as how different factors affect the intended nonparticipation or participation variable of the rural poor in MFIs, logistic regression analysis was employed. Generally, it was looked at estimating the conditional expectations of continuous variables as in regression or at estimating distributions (Gujarati, Porter & Gunasaker, 2012). In modeling logistic regression, conditional probabilities used to be scrutinized. There are many situations where one might be interested in observing the input-output relationships, as in regression, but the output variable would be discrete rather than continuous. Thus, logistic regression analysis is used to predicting the relationships between a criterion variable (dependent variable) and several predictor variables (independent variables) when dependent variable is discrete rather than continuous (Cooper & Schindler, 2006; Pallant, 2007).

Logistic regression is employed as a descriptive tool in several types of conditions. Firstly, it is used in the application of regression analysis in the case of binary (such as "yes" or "no") outcomes. Secondly, in addition to binary outcome, some input variables may or may not be continuous. It has descriptive application which calls for controlling for confounding variables to better evaluate the contribution of other variables. A third use of logistic regression is to test and explain probability distribution theories. In this approach, logistic regression is used to describe an entire structure of linkages that have been from a probabilistic theory. In addition to being a descriptive tool, logistic regression is also utilized as an inference tool to test hypotheses and to fit a stochastic model (Cooper & Schindler 2006).

Suppose the binary outcomes are for "yes" it is "1" and the other is "0" for "no". It doesn't matter if it is coded as 0 for "yes", and 1 for "no". If Y becomes an indicator variable, it can be shown that Pr(Y = 1) = E[Y]. Similarly, Pr(Y = 1|X = x) = E[Y|X = x]. In short, conditional probability is the conditional expectation of the indicator. This is helpful, because by this point one may know all about estimating conditional expectations. The most straightforward thing at this point would be to pick out the favorite smoother and estimate the regression function for the indicator variable; this will be an estimate of the conditional probability function. There are two reasons not for executing that idea. One is that probabilities must be between 0 and 1, but the smoothers will not necessarily respect that, even if all the observed Y_i they get are either 0 or 1. The other is that it might be better off making more use of trying to estimate probabilities, by more explicitly modeling the probability (Pallant, 2007).

Assume that Pr(Y = 1|X = x) = p(x ; θ), for some function p parameterized by θ. parameterized function θ, and further assume that observations are independent of each other (Gujarati, Porter & Gunasaker, 2012). The (conditional) likelihood function is:

$$\Pi \Pr(Y= y|\, X= x) = \Pi\ p(x\ ;\ \theta)^{y}\ (1 - p\ (x\ ;\theta)^{1-y}$$

Notably, in a sequence of Bernoulli trials y_1, ... y_n, where there is a constant probability of success p, the likelihood is:

$$\Pi\ p^{y}\ (1 - p)^{1-y}$$

An explanation of logistic regression begins with an explanation of the logistic function. The logistic function is useful, because it can take an input with any value from negative to positive infinity, whereas the output always takes values between zero and one and hence is interpretable as a probability (Anderson, Sweeney & Williams, 2008). The logistic function σ *(t)* is defined as follows:

$$\sigma(t) = \frac{e^t}{e^t + 1} = \frac{1}{1 + e^{-t}},$$

A graph of the logistic function is shown in Figure 4.3.

If ***t*** is viewed as a linear function of an explanatory variable x(or of a linear combination of explanatory variables), then we express *t* as follows:

$$t = \beta_0 + \beta_1 x$$

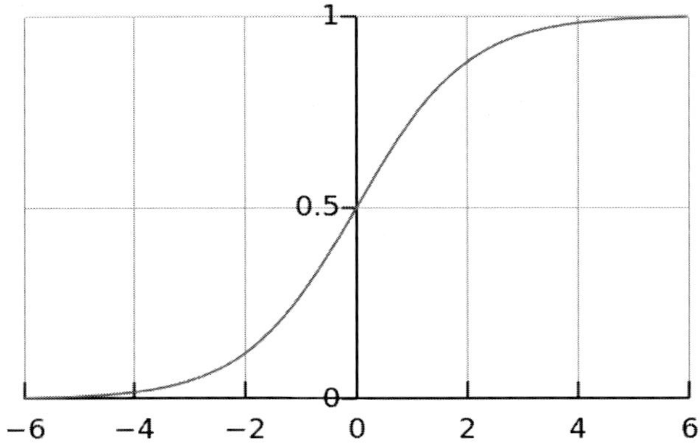

Source: Anderson, Sweeney & Williams (2008).

Figure 4.3. The *logistic function* σ (t): (σ (t) ε [0, 1] for all t.

And the logistic function can now be written as:

$$F(x) = \frac{1}{1 + e^{-(\beta_0 + \beta_1 x)}}$$

Notably, *F(x)* is interpreted as the probability of the dependent variable equaling a "success" or "case" rather than a failure or non-case. It's clear that the response variables Y_i are not identically distributed: $P(Y_i = 1 \mid X)$ differs from one data point X_i to another, though they are independent given design matrix *X* and shared with parameters β. It can now be defined the inverse of the logistic function, *g*, the Logit (log odds) as:

$$g(F(x)) = \ln \frac{F(x)}{1 - F(x)} = \beta_0 + \beta_1 x,$$

And equivalently:

$$\frac{F(x)}{1 - F(x)} = e^{\beta_0 + \beta_1 x}.$$

Where,

- *g(.)* refers to the logit function. The equation for *g (F(x))* illustrates that the logit (i.e., log-odds or natural logarithm of the odds) is equivalent to the linear regression expression.
- *In* denotes the natural logarithm.
- *F(X)* is the probability that the dependent variable equals a case, given some linear combination *X* of the predictors. The formula for *F(X)* illustrates that the probability of the dependent variable equaling a case is equal to the value of the logistic function of the linear regression expression. This is important in that it shows that the value of the linear regression expression can vary from negative to positive infinity and yet, after transformation, the resulting expression for the probability *F(x)* ranges between 0 and 1.
- β_0 is the intercept from the linear regression equation (the value of the criterion when the predictor is equal to zero).
- $\beta_1 x$ is the regression coefficient multiplied by some value of the predictor.
- Base *e* denotes the exponential function (Anderson, Sweeney & Williams, 2008).

In gist, *Y* is a binary variable and the conditional probability $Pr(Y = 1|X = x)$ as a function of *x*; any unknown parameters in the function are to be estimated by maximum likelihood. By now, it will not be surprising to learn that statisticians may have approached this problem by asking "how can linear regression be used to solve this?" In answering this question, the following points can be mentioned:

1. The most obvious idea is to let *p(x)* be a linear function of *x*. Every increment of a component of *x* would add or subtract so much to the probability. The conceptual problem here is that p must be between *0* and 1 and linear functions are unbounded. Moreover, in many situations we empirically see "diminishing returns" — changing *p* by the same amount requires a bigger change in *x* when *p* is already large (or small) than when *p* is close to 1/2. Linear models can't do this.
2. The next most obvious idea is to let *log p(x)* be a linear function of *x*, so that changing an input variable multiplies the probability by a fixed amount. The problem is that logarithms are unbounded in only one direction and linear functions are not.
3. Finally, the easiest modification of *log p* which has an unbounded range is the logistic (or logit) transformation, *log [p/(1−p)]*. One can make this a linear function of *x* without fear of nonsensical results (Anderson, Sweeney & Williams, 2008).

Thus, the last alternative is logistic regression.

The odds of the dependent variable equaling a case (given some linear combination x of the predictors) are equivalent to the exponential function of the linear regression expression. This illustrates how the logit serves as a link function between the probability and the linear regression expression. Given that the logit ranges between negative and positive infinity, it provides an adequate criterion upon which to conduct linear regression and the logit is easily converted back into the odds. So we define odds of the dependent variable equaling a case (given some linear combination x of the predictors) as follows ((Anderson, Sweeney & Williams, 2008):

$$\text{odds} = e^{\beta_0+\beta_1 x}.$$

The odds ratio can be defined as:

$$OR = \text{odds}(x+1)/\,\text{odds}(x) = \frac{\frac{F(x+1)}{1-F(x+1)}}{\frac{F(x)}{1-F(x)}} =$$

$$= e^{\beta_0+\beta_1(x+1)}/e^{\beta_0+\beta_1 x} = e^{\beta_1}$$

Or for binary variable *F(0)* instead of *F(x)* and *F(1)* for *F(x+1)*. This exponential relationship provides an interpretation for β_1. The odds are multiplied by $e^{\beta 1}$ *for* every 1 unit increase in x (Anderson, Sweeney, Williams, 2008).

If there are multiple explanatory variables, the above expression $\beta_0 + \beta_1 x$ can be revised to $\beta_0 + \beta_1 x_1 + \beta_2 x_2 + \ldots + \beta_m x_m$. Then when this is used in the equation relating the logged odds of a success to the values of the predictors, the linear regression will be a multiple regression with *m* explanatory variables; the parameters β_j for all $j = 0, 1, 2, \ldots, m$ are all estimated.

4.8. Chapter Summary

This chapter describes research framework, research hypotheses and research design. It also discusses how the study examines the measurement of dependent and several independent variables. The sampling and data collection procedures along with the data analytical techniques are delineated briefly in details. As the study includes the TPB as its underlying conceptual framework, it will test the different hypotheses related to its internal as well as external variables that affect the nonparticipation or participation of the rural poor in MFIs in Bangladesh. The findings and the interpretations of the study based on logistic and multiple linear regression analyses are provided in the next chapter 5.

Chapter 5

FINDINGS OF THE STUDY

5.1. INTRODUCTION

The prime objective of the study is to predict on the factors that directly or indirectly can influence the participation or nonparticipation of the rural poor in MFIs in Bangladesh. To attain this objective, the study conducted a survey in six different regions in Bangladesh with a closed-ended questionnaire to collect the relevant information from the nonparticipants and participants in MFIs. The study has formulated thirteen hypotheses to examine the factors that are potential to influence the nonparticipation or participation of the rural poor in microfinance programs.

The survey was conducted interviewing 450 respondents in these regions and collected 450 data. While among 450 data, some were mistakenly erroneous and not usable for the analysis, ultimately 420 were found usable. Among the data, there are 280 respondents who are observed to be nonparticipants and 140 respondents who are participants. The study employs logistic and linear multiple regression analyses for identifying the reasons of nonparticipation in MFIs in Bangladesh. In the following section, the results of these analyses are presented.

5.2. Results Discussion

5.2.1. Logistic Regression Analysis

In the research models, three variables, attitude, subjective norms and PBC which influence intention toward actual behavior of nonparticipation of the rural poor in MFIs were shown. Besides, eight explanatory variables are presumed to be potential barriers to influence actual behavior of nonparticipation in MFIs in Bangladesh. Based on this conception, the study first employed the logistic regression analysis and then multiple linear regressions in order to test the hypotheses postulated for the study. As the dependent variable (nonparticipation or participation) has been set with a single question whether the rural poor participate in MFIs or not, SEM cannot be applicable. Besides, as the variable is dichotomous in characteristics, logistic regression has been done to examine the factors that can influence it. However, the results of these analyses are provided in the following section starting with the characteristics of the respondents.

5.2.2. Characteristics of the Study Participants

Table 5.13 displays the characteristics of the survey respondents, including gender, age, marital status, education, yearly household income, amount of land and other assets. In terms of gender, the majority of the respondents were female (86.2%). As to age, most of the respondents were 26-40 years old (56.4%), followed by 41-55 years old (23.1%), then 15-25 (11.2%) and 56-60 (9.3%). Majority of the study respondents were married (89.3%), single (9.3%) and divorced (1.7%).

Education of the survey respondents was relatively skewed over four groups, including totally illiterate and primary school (64%), high school (26..7%), college degree (5.5%) and bachelor (3.8%). Income of the survey respondents varied, including USD 1001 to USD 1400 (27.6%), followed by more than USD 1401 (26.2%), USD 571 to 1000 (23.6%), then USD 285 or less (11.0%), and USD 286 to USD 570 (11.6%).

As the rural areas of Bangladesh particularly in the northern region are poor in terms of educational and communication infrastructure, literacy rate is very low. Yet income generating activities other than agriculture are scanty. For this reason, the rural poor are mostly dependent on rickshaw-pulling and cattle-cart driving which generate poor income level for them (CARE, 2005).

In terms of land owned by the respondents, the majority of them were marginal land-owners (36.9%) who possessed from 1decimal to 33 decimal of land, followed by landless (25%), then 34 to 66 decimal of land (20%), 67 to 100 decimal (9.3%) and more than one acre of land (8.8%). As to other assets, the majority of the respondents (60.2%) who owned the asset of USD 285 or less, followed by (21%) who owned more than USD 1401 of asset, then USD 570 to 1000 of asset (7.6%), also USD 1000 to 1400 (6.7%) and USD 286 to 570 (4.5%).

Overall, socio-demographic results of this study reflected previous participatory behavioral research in the area of gender (Brown & Morrison, 2003; McGehee, 2002), age (Coghlan, 2008; McIntosh & Zahra, 2007; Stoddart & Rogerson, 2004), education (McGehee, 2002; Stoddart & Rogerson, 2004), and income and other assets (Brown & Morrison, 2003; Coghlan, 2008; Stoddart & Rogerson, 2004). The number of participants who participated in MFIs before were 229 (54.5%). Among them 191 respondents never participated in MFIs (45.5%). Among the respondents the number of participants in MFIs is 140 (33.3%) and nonparticipants are 280 (66.7%).

5.2.3. Descriptive Statistics of the Study Constructs

Table 5.1 presents the means and standard deviations of all the variables in the study.

On average, respondents estimated their attitudes toward the rural poor participation in MFIs in positive sentiment that ranged from moderate to simple agreement. All the largest mean values of the factors are taken in favor of the conclusion.

Table 5.1. Descriptive Statistics for Constructs

Construct	N	Minimum	Maximum	Mean	SD
1. Nonparticipation	420	1.00	2.00	1.6667	.47197
2. Intention	420	1.00	4.40	3.0986	.36257
3. Attitude	420	1.00	4.25	3.4558	.28248
4. Subjective Norms	420	1.00	8.67	1.5778	.45425
5. PBC	420	1.00	5.00	4.4437	.28064
6. Fear of Risk	420	1.00	5.00	3.1595	.77600
7. Individual Preference	420	1.00	4.60	2.4562	.51301
8. Religion	420	1.25	5.00	4.1107	.83425
9. Female Head	420	1.00	5.00	4.1175	.80995
10. Friends' Advice	420	1.00	5.00	3.1202	.64010
11. Resource	420	1.00	5.00	3.2940	.72327
12. Knowledge	420	1.00	5.00	3.5083	1.13640
13. Ill-Health	420	1.00	5.00	3.8151	.77855

5.2.4. Correlation Analysis

The correlation analyses showed that each sub-dimension and each construct were somewhat correlated with one another (Table 5.15). Specifically, the variables which showed negative correlations with others, these results were consistent with the results of subsequent analyses. There are some correlation coefficients which are statistically significant. For example, the variables of intention and nonparticipation were observed to have a high negative correlation (-0.23) and significant at 0.01 level of significance. The correlation between nonparticipation and attitude is (-0.16) and significant at 0.01 level of significance. Fear and intention (-0.27) and insufficiency of resources and fear (0.15) were also observed to be significant at 0.01. As such there are a few other coefficients which are also found to be statistically significant. These results were consistent with the path analysis and direction.

There were some coefficients which showed negative as well as positive correlations. Though some correlations were not very high in their absolute value, they were significant at 0.01 level. Among them, there were many variables which had very low correlations and not statistically significant as well. These outcomes were consistent with other analyses of SEM and logistic regression.

Table 5.2. Correlation Coefficient of the Main Constructs

	1	2	3	4	5	6	7	8	9	10	11	12
1 Nonparticip.	1											
2. Intention	-.23**	1										
3. Attitude	-.16**	-.001	1									
4. SN	-.02	-.03	-.08	1								
5. PBC	-.01	.03	.03	-.19**	1							
6. Fear	-.12	.05	.42**	-.02	.01	1						
7. Preference	.05	-.02	.04	.06	.03	.19**	1					
8. Religion	-.27**	.13*	.46**	.01	.04	.47**	.12*	1				
9. Female	.09	.02	.24**	-.01	-.02	.18**	.03	.24**	1			
10. Friend	.07	-.07	.09	-.08	-.04	.09	.13**	.01	.08	1		
11. Resource	-.03	-.17**	-.21**	-.03	-.04	-.31**	-.10*	-.12*	-.12*	-.14**	1	
12. Knowledge	-.02	.14**	-.01	-.01	.02	.00	-.03	.11*	-.14**	-.12*	.34**	1
13. Ill-health	.15**	.06	-.10*	.01	.02	-.07	-.13**	.04	-.08	-.07	.28**	.41**

Note: ** indicate significance at .01 level; * indicates significance at .05 level.

There were many correlation coefficients that were very low in absolute numbers with positive and negative signs. These were not statistically significant. This meant there were no correlations between the respective variables of incorporated in the research model. These results also appeared to be consistent with the results obtained in logistic and multiple regression analyses.

5.2.5. Overall Impression of the Respondents about the Microfinance Programs

Despite the claim of the success of the NGO-MFIs in Bangladesh in delivering microfinance to poor rural women and bringing socioeconomic changes to many of the households, the present study finds (during data collection) that there are still many borrowers who become vulnerable and trapped by the microfinance system (Karim, 2011). At the grass-root level of microfinance operation, the NGO-MFIs and the peer group members impose an intense pressure on borrowers for making timely loan repayment rather than working to raise collective responsibility and women-empowerment as originally envisaged by the GB (Rahman, 2001; Yunus, 1997).

There had been many borrowers in rural Bangladesh who maintain the regularity of loan repayment schedule by loan recycling process (paying off older loans by acquiring new ones) which significantly increases borrowers' debt-liability (Karim, 2011). The institutional debt-burden on the rural poor households adds to mental anguish and tension among the members of the households and creates new forms of institutional dominance over the poor clients of the MFIs. Thus, the qualitative scrutiny of this study questions about the conventional perception of microfinance programs and about the orthodox view of the success and women-empowerment in society (Rahman, 2001).

As this study was based on exploratory research techniques, diverse qualitative information about demographic, socio-economic and emotional condition were collected through a comprehensive household survey of interviewing the nonparticipants and the participants in the MFIs in Bangladesh. Particularly, emotional feelings of the rural poor about the MF participation were more carefully recorded as emotion plays a positive role in decision making, creativity and relationship building with an organization (Leary, Pillemer & Wheeler, 2013). While data collection was primarily devoted to gather information through closed-ended structured questionnaire, the interviewers were attentive to document the observations and experiences of the respondents' about group-based lending system of the NGO-MFIs in the study areas.

Many nonparticipants and participants in MFIs informed that they did not like the group-based lending system. Rather they liked to have loans on an individual basis. They also did not like the weekly repayment system as well because of the inherent risk in failing to repay off the loans. To make this point clear, one of the respondents provided an example from a neighboring GB branch in northern Bangladesh where a woman failed to pay installments and accidentally died. Having got information about that incident, the bank workers rushed to her home and asked her family-members to pay back the loans. The bank workers were insisting that the loans must be repaid before the burial of the body of the deceased. Such types of instances were not uncommon to all other areas of Bangladesh (Karim, 2011).

Many respondents expressed their deep concern about the rate of the interest charged by the MFIs. In their opinion, the rate of interest was much higher than regular bank rates. When the interviewer asked them why they took loans from those MFIs despite these high rates, in response they replied that necessity knew no bound. In fact, they disliked paying the interest in exchange of credit. In this respect, rural villagers mentioned that the religious leaders frequently advised them not to take loans from any NGOs or MFIs, because interest is forbidden in the religion. These types of instances were also mentioned by Karim (2011) in her study. For this reason, many informants expressed their moral support in favor of IMFIs. However, the problem is, IMFIs are not available in every locality of the rural areas of Bangladesh.

There have been many other instances in rural Bangladesh which include the case of breaking houses in order to recover the loans by selling the tins and woods of the houses. This type of instance was also mentioned by Rahman (2001) and Karim (2011) in their studies. According to many respondents in the present study areas, there are two types of pressure imposed on the defaulters of the borrowers. One is from the NGO-MFIs and the other is from the members of the borrowing group. The members of the borrowing group inflict pressure, because due to a single default in a group the further loans won't be approved for the default group. In such a situation, the defaulters become highly vulnerable in terms of losing social prestige (*ijjat*) as well as other fixed assets such as houses including other household utensils. Thus, friends and relatives of the rural poor used to advise them not to take any loans from the MFIs in Bangladesh.

5.2.6. Results of the Model Analyses

As the present study employed two types of analytical techniques namely the logistic regression and the multiple regression analyses, Model

1 and Model 2 were analyzed using logistic regression technique. In the following section, the results of logistic regression are presented:

Logistic Regression Analyses

Logistic regression is a flexible method of data analysis that is appropriate whenever a quantitative variable (the dependent or criterion variable) is to be examined in relationship to any other factors (expressed as independent or predictor variables). Relationships may be nonlinear, independent variables may be quantitative or qualitative and one can examine the effects of a single variable or multiple variables with or without the effects of other variables taken into account (Cohen, Cohen, West & Aiken, 2003).

In its simplest form, logistic regression can be used to analyze the relationship between a binary (1, 0) dependent variable and a number of independent variables. There has been a difference between logistic regression and ordinary regression. In logistic regression, an estimate of the probability of a case belonging to a particular group is provided in order to represent the statistical significance of the independent variables included in the model.

The logistic regression model was run in this study which aims to identify the barriers which are responsible for predicting participation and nonparticipation in MFIs in Bangladesh. Of 420 respondents who were interviewed in collecting data, 280 respondents were nonparticipants and 140 participants. The logistic regression equation was run for estimating the selected eight external factors that can influence nonparticipation in MFIs where the sample (n = 420) represented both groups of the participants and the nonparticipants.

Based on the analysis done by the logistic regression and multiple linear regressions, the study evaluated six different models by estimating the variables by which the study hypotheses were examined statistically. Among theses six different models, there are two models that employ logistic regression because both the models use dichotomous dependent variable of nonparticipation of the rural poor in MFIs in Bangladesh. The results of the logistic regression (Model 1 and Model 2) and the multiple regressions are presented in the following section. However, it starts with the results of two logistic models (Model 1 and Model 2). As stated earlier, Model 1 incorporates all the variables including the demographic factors and then Model 2 incorporates only the external factors to influence the dependent variable of nonparticipation. The results of Model 1 are represented in the following section.

Model 1

The results of the logistic regression equation (Model 1) are presented in Tables 5.3 and 5.4. The logistic regression output includes a classification table (Table 5.3) which can be used to evaluate the effectiveness of the estimated model in correctly classifying the individuals in the sample group. This table is compiled by estimating the probability of each individual reporting nonparticipating in MFIs and classifying them into the appropriate group. The default probability for group classification is 0.5. Thus, in this instance, of the 280 individuals who reported that they did not participate in MFIs, and 38 (86.40 per cent) were correctly classified by the model. Similarly, 140 of the 90 (87.10 per cent) who reported that participated in MFIs were also correctly classified. Therefore, of the total sample of 420 individuals surveyed, 79.00 per cent could be correctly classified as either reporting that they participated or did not participate in MFIs by the estimated model comprising just eight independent variables.

Table 5.3 demonstrates the results of logistic regression analyses representing odds ratios along with the significance of the coefficients of independent variables. In the Table, the results show that among the individual respondents' demographic features such as age, marital status, education, income, land and asset, two variables such as age and marital status are observed not to have any impact statistically on the dependent variable of nonparticipation in MFIs. However, rest of the four variables such as education, income, land and asset are observed to be statistically significant to impact on nonparticipation variable. Among these four variables, two exhibit negative impacts on the dependent variable of nonparticipation and the other two have positive impacts. The individuals who are more educated there is 79% more probability to be nonparticipants in MFIs.

Table 5.3. Classification Values of the Survey (Model 1)

	Observed		Predicted		
			Nonparticipation		Percentage Correct
			1	0	
Step 1	Nonparticipation	1	38	242	86.4
		0	90	50	64.3
	Overall Percentage				79.0

Note: The cut value is .500.

Table 5.4. Determinants of Nonparticipation in MFIs, Dependent Variable: Nonparticipation (Yes = 1, No = 0)

Independent Variables	Coefficient	Significance	Exp(B)
Age	-.248	.226	.780
Marital status	-.864	.127	.422
Education	.583**	.010	1.791
Income	-.468**	.001	.626
Amount of land	-.262*	.037	.770
Asset	.274**	.005	1.316
Intention	-.552**	.001	.576
Attitude	.016	.938	1.016
SN	-.003	.976	.997
PBC	-.711**	.000	.491
Fear of risk associated with loans	-.058	.754	.944
Individual preference	-.119	.582	.888
Religious leaders' lecture	-1.199**	.000	.301
Female head of household	.430**	.012	1.696
Friends' advice	.205	.301	1.227
Insufficiency of resources	-.129	.451	.879
Lack of business knowledge	-.205	.170	.815
Ill-health or vulnerability to crisis	.218	.178	1.243
Constant	11.672**	.000	.0117
- 2 Log Likelihood †	356.337		
Model Chi-square	178.335		.000
Percent correctly predicted	79		
N	420		

Note: * = significant at 5 percent level; ** = significant at 1 percent level.

† The *log-likelihood* is the expression that maximizes to determine optimal values of the estimated coefficients (β). Log-likelihood values cannot be used alone as an index of fit because they are a function of sample size but can be used to compare the fit of different coefficients.

Similarly, more assets increase the probability of nonparticipation of the rural poor in MFIs by more than 31%. However, income and land have been observed to have a negative impact on the probability of nonparticipation. This result is contrasting against the previous results obtained by Ashraf (2011c).

Of the four internal variables of TPB model such as intention, attitude, SN and PBC, only intention and PBC appear to be statistically significant to influence the behavioral variable of nonparticipation of the village poor in MFIs. Interestingly, both the variables are observed to have negative impacts on nonparticipation variable. This result implies that intention and PBC of the rural poor reduce the probability of nonparticipation in MFIs in Bangladesh. Evidently, this outcome appears contrary to the previous study by Ashraf (2011c).

Among the external independent variables only two (religious leaders' lectures and spousal dislike of female head of households) are observed to be important to influence nonparticipation in MFIs. Dubiously, the variable of religious leaders' lectures has a negative impact on nonparticipation and this result is also contrary to the findings of Ashraf (2011c). However, spousal dislike to female head of household has a positive statistical impact on nonparticipation. This outcome implies that spousal dislike to female head of households increases the probability of nonparticipation in MFIs of the rural poor in Bangladesh by about 70%. This evidence appears to be similar to the previous studies (Ashraf, 2011c).

Table 5.5. Classification Values of the Survey (Model 2)

	Observed		Predicted		
			Nonparticipation		Percentage
			1	0	Correct
Step 1	Nonparticipation	1	36	244	87.1
		0	49	91	35.0
	Overall Percentage				69.8

Note: The Cut Value is .500.

Model 2

The results of the logistic regression equation (Model 2) are presented in Table 5.6 and Table 5.7. The logistic regression output includes a classification table (Table 5.6) which can be used to assess the effectiveness of the estimated model in correctly classifying the individuals in the sample group. This table is compiled by estimating the probability of each individual reporting nonparticipating in MFIs and classifying them into the appropriate group. The default probability for group classification is 0.5. Thus, in this instance, of the 140 individuals who reported that they participated in MFIs, and 49 (35.00 per cent) were correctly classified by the model. Similarly, 280 of the 244 (87.10 per cent) who reported that they did not participate in MFIs were also correctly classified. Therefore, of the total sample of 420 individuals surveyed, 69.80 per cent could be correctly classified as either reporting that they participated or did not participate in MFIs by the estimated model comprising just eight independent variables.

Regression results of the Model 2, which excluded demographic variables, have been represented in Table 5.7 below incorporating only external variables affecting the dichotomous variable of nonparticipation in MFIs. Of the eight explanatory variables, five were observed to be statistically significant in influencing nonparticipation of the village poor in MFIs in Bangladesh. Among the five independent variables, three variables were found to be statistically significant at 0.01 level. They were religious leaders' lecture (β = -1.033), female head of household (β = .528), and poor health or vulnerability to crises (β = .580). Two other variables were found to be statistically significant at 0.05 level. They were individual preference (β = .516) and insufficiency of resources (β = -.311). Three variables i.e., fear of risk, friend's advice, and lacks of knowledge were not statistically significant. The result appeared to be consistent with that of other studies such as Zohir (2001), Huq (2001) and Evans et al. 1999).

The estimation results of the logistic model have been presented in Table 5.7. The model chi-square value (66.353) and the significance level of 0.000 indicate that hypothesis that the coefficients of all the variables in the model are zero cannot be rejected at better than 99 percent level. In the estimated model, five variables excluding constant are found statistically significant and the model on the whole can predict 70 percent of the cases correctly.

Table 5.6. Determinants (external variables) of Nonparticipation in MFIs, Dependent Variable: Nonparticipation (Yes = 1, No = 0)

Independent Variables	Coefficient	Significance	Exp(B)
Fear of getting into risk of loans	-.127	.462	.881
Individual preference	.516*	.033	1.676
Religious leaders' lecture	-1.033**	.000	.356
Female head of household	.528**	.001	1.696
Friends' advice	.200	.273	1.221
Insufficiency of resources	-.311*	.046	.733
Lack of business knowledge	-.025	.836	.975
Ill-health or vulnerability to crisis	.580**	.000	1.786
Constant	.336	.807	1.399
- 2 Log Likelihood†	468.319		
Model Chi-square	66.353		.000
Percent correctly predicted	69.8		
N	420		

Note: * = significant at 5 percent level; ** = significant at 1 percent level.

† The *log-likelihood* is the expression that maximizes to determine optimal values of the estimated coefficients (β). *Log-likelihood* values cannot be used alone as an index of fit because they are a function of sample size but can be used to compare the fit of different coefficients.

Table 5.7. Determinants of Intention toward Nonparticipation in MFIs

Variables	Unstandardized Coefficients		Standardized Coefficients		
	B	S.E	Beta	t-value	Sig.
Constant	.551	.199		20.762	.006
Attitude	.733	.043	.642	17.115	.000
Subjective norms (SN)	000	.033	000	.023	.981
Perceived behavioral control (PBC)	.045	.038	.049	1.182	.238

Note: $R^2 = .415$, Adj. $R^2 = .411$, $F(3,416) = 98.26$, $p < .000$, $n = 420$, DV: Intention.

Estimated coefficients and odds ratios of the variables revealed a number of interesting aspects of nonparticipation of the rural poor in MFIs. Though the factor of fear of getting into risk of loans is not observed to be statistically significant to influence its odds, it is obvious to demonstrate that the nonparticipation reduces 88 percent or increases the participation of the rural poor in MFIs by about 12 percent (i.e., 1.00 - 0.881).

The variable of individual preference is found to be statistically significant at 5 percent level of significance. The odds ratio pertaining to this factor is observed to be 1.676 which means that individual preference of the rural poor increases about 68 percent nonparticipation in MFIs in Bangladesh.

The result of odds ratio of the religious leaders' lecture was observed to be .356 which indicates that this factor reduces the probability of nonparticipation by 35 percent. The factor of female head of household increases the probability of nonparticipation by 70 percent. Similarly, friend's negative advice increases the probability of nonparticipation by 22 percent.

Insufficiency of resources reduces the probability of participation by 27 percent. Similarly, lack of business knowledge reduces probability of participation by 3 percent. Ill-health or vulnerability to crises increases the probability of nonparticipation by 79 percent.

Multiple Regression Analyses

As mentioned in previous section that apart from the logistic regression, the study used the multiple regression technique for evaluating the hypotheses formulated in the earlier section based on TPB as its theoretical framework. There have been five models such as Model 3, Model 4, Model 5 and Model 6 based on different constructs of TPB for evaluating the hypotheses H_2, H_3, H_4, H_5, H_6, H_7, H_8, H_9, H_{10}, H_{11}, H_{12} and H_{13} following statistical criteria. In this section, the evaluation of these hypotheses based on the results of multiple regression analyses has been presented. This analysis is based on the hypotheses constructed incorporating the Model 3, 4, 5 and 6. The analyses also focus on the interpretations of the outcomes in comparison to previous studies done in the domain of microfinance participation and nonparticipation in the context of rural Bangladesh.

Model 3

In the Table 5.8, the estimated results of the multiple regression with intention as dependent variable are presented. The antecedents of the intention variable are attitude, SN and PBC. Among these three variables, only one variable of attitude is observed to be positively statistically significant to influence intention ($p < .000$) toward nonparticipation of the rural poor in MFIs in Bangladesh. This result is supported by previous studies done by Ashraf (2011c), Karim (2011), Evans et al. (1999), Mahmud (2000) and many others mentioned in the section of literature review. This outcome implies that attitude of the rural poor in Bangladesh increases their intended nonparticipation in MFIs which reflected in the recent decline in growth of MFIs in Bangladesh.

Model 4

The estimated results of the Model 4 is represented in Table 5.9. In the Model, attitude is used as dependent variable which has two immediate antecedents to influence on intended nonparticipation of the village poor in MFIs. Among the two variables of fear of risks associated with loans and individual preference, only fear of risks associated with loans is observed to be negatively statistically significant to influence attitude toward intended nonparticipation of the rural poor in MFIs. This result is substantially consistent with the previous studies done in the field of microfinance literature which explore the facts of nonparticipation in MFIs in Bangladesh. The studies accomplished by Ashraf (2011c), Dyal-Chand (2007), Evans et al. (1999), Karim (2011) and Rahman (1999) are a few to name. As there are many instances in which the rural poor off and on were harassed by the officers of MFIs in the case of default in loan repayment, village people especially women-folk are reluctant to be involved in microfinance programs.

Table 5.8. Determinants of Attitude toward Intended Nonparticipation in MFIs

Variables	Unstandardized Coefficients		Standardized Coefficients	t-value	Sig.
	B	S.E	Beta		
Constant	5.289	.205	-	25.779	.006
Fear of risks associated with loans	-.733	.043	-.642	-17.115	.000
Individual preference	000	.033	000	.023	.981

Note: $R^2 = .17$, Adj. $R^2 = .166$, $F(2,417) = 42.717$, $p < .000$, $n = 420$, DV: Attitude.

Model 5

Table 5.9. Determinants of Subjective Norms toward Intended Nonparticipation in MFIs

Variables	Unstandardized Coefficients		Standardized Coefficients	t-value	Sig.
	B	S.E	Beta		
Constant	3.916	.479	-	8.178	.000
Religious leaders' lectures	-.048	.080	-030	-.600	.549
Female head of households	-.124	.077	-.082	-1.616	.100
Friends' negative advice	.012	.092	.007	.132	.895

Note: $R^2 = .009$, Adj. $R^2 = .001$, $F(3,416) = 1.197$, $p > .000$, $n = 420$, DV: SN.

Table 5.10 represents the estimated results of the Model 5 which incorporated subjective norms as dependent variable whose immediate antecedents are the social referents such as religious leaders' lectures, spousal dislike of female head of households and friends' negative advice. Of these three variables, only one variable of spousal dislike of female head of household has been observed to be negatively statistically significant to influence subjective norms toward intended nonparticipation of the rural poor in MFIs in Bangladesh. This result is highly consistent with the previous studies such as Ashraf (2011c), Evans et al. (1999) Mahmud (2000) and others. As the oriental social culture is tilted toward male dominated family environment, female as the head of households is disliked by the spouse. Thus, it has an important negative impact on subjective norms that influence intended nonparticipation of the poor in MFIs.

Model 6

The last Model 6 which incorporates PBC as the dependent variable and its immediate antecedents are insufficient resources possessed by the borrowers, their lack of business knowledge and poor health or vulnerability to crises. The estimated results of the regression are represented in the Table 5.11. Among the three external variables, only one i.e., lack of business knowledge of the borrowers is observed to be negatively statistically significant to influence PBC toward intended nonparticipation of the village poor in MFIs in Bangladesh. As the rural poor in Bangladesh are mostly illiterate, they have very limited business knowledge by which profitable business initiative can be undertaken. This particular aspect knowledge and business skills of the rural borrowers hinders the rate of return in the business for which they take loans. Therefore, in the end these borrowers become failed to repay their loans in right time and right amount. This implies that lack of business knowledge of the borrowers is another impediment to participation in MFIs.

Table 5.10. Determinants of PBC toward Intended Nonparticipation in MFIs

Variables	Unstandardized Coefficients		Standardized Coefficients		
	B	S.E	Beta	t-value	Sig.
Constant	2.276	.311	-	8.178	.000
Insufficient resources	.371	.058	.299	6.396	.000
Lack of knowledge	-.083	.051	-.083	-1.631	.100
Ill-health	.034	.059	.030	.585	.559

Note: $R^2 = .098$, Adj. $R^2 = .091$, $F(3,416) = 14.987$, $p < .000$, $n = 420$, DV: PBC.

5.2.7. Hypotheses and Test Results Interpretations

There have been thirteen hypotheses in total for this study formulated earlier based on the different constructs of the TPB model including eight external factors those have potential impacts on nonparticipation and participation or the rural poor in MFIs in the context of Bangladesh. Now in the following section, those hypotheses have been evaluated in the light of statistical principles.

This section also interpreted the study findings in relation to each of the research hypotheses. It also covered implications derived from the study findings, followed by limitations of the study, and concluded with suggestions for the alternatives of conventional MFIs presently operating in Bangladesh.

Hypothesis 1: Intention is Positively Related with Nonparticipation in MFIs .

From the results of Model 1 analyzed by employing logistic regression with dichotomous dependent variable of nonparticipation (Table 5.5), it is evident that the coefficient of intention appears to be -.545, $p < .000$ and its odd ration is .580. This means that intention was significantly and negatively related with nonparticipation. This also means that intention decreases nonparticipation by 58 percent and increases the participation of the borrowers by 42 percent. Thus, it is evident that hypothesis 1 is not accepted.

Hypothesis 2: Attitude is Positively Related with Intention toward Nonparticipation in MFIs.

Hypothesis 2 that attitude and intention toward nonparticipation in MFIs are positively related was observed to be accepted. That means attitude and intention were statistically significantly related with each other ((adjusted R^2 = .411, β = 0.642, $p < .000$, t = 17.128 and F [3, 416] = 98.26, $p < .000$. Hence, attitude was highly positively related with intention toward nonparticipation.

Thus, the result was consistent with other studies that deal with TPB in different contexts of empirical analysis such as Lee (2011), Lee and Moscrado (2005), Lam and Hsu (2004), Zini (2002). In the original theory testing of TPB, similar results were obtained (Ajzen, 1991). In this regard, the theory of TPB was reconfirmed that it validated the original claim of positive link between attitude and behavior in question.

Hypothesis 3: Subjective Norms are Positively Related with Intention toward Nonparticipation in MFIs.

Hypotheses 3 that subjective norms and intention toward nonparticipation in MFIs were observed to be statistically insignificant. The results reveled that subjective norms (adjusted $R^2 = .002$, $\beta = .029$, $p > .05$, $p = 0.554$, $t = 0.593$, $F\ [1, 418] = 0.351$) was not significantly related with intention toward nonparticipation in MFIs It was believed that the social pressure groups that asserted subjective norms, including family members, relatives and friends, influenced the decision making process for the survey respondents who were not interested in participating in MFIs. Hence, the hypothesis 3 was not supported by the evidence.

This finding was not consistent with previous other related research that found that social pressure groups had a positive impact on the decisions to intention toward nonparticipation behavior (Lam & Hsu, 2006; Oh & Hsu, 2001; Phetvaroon, 2006). For example, Lam and Hsu (2006) found that Taiwanese tourists traveling to Hong Kong were influenced by their social pressure groups, including family members and friends. Phetvaroon (2006) found that subjective norms, including family members and friends, were the strongest factor that influenced making a decision to visit Phuket, Thailand.

Perhaps most importantly, in the context of participation or nonparticipation research, this finding did not support previous research rejecting the influence of family members, friends, and relatives on participation in a variety of participatory activities (Deery et al., 1998; McGehee & Santos, 2005; McGehee, 2002; Stoddart & Rogerson, 2004).

The possible reasons behind this contradictory research results were perhaps present in the socio-economic and demographic characteristics of the respondents of this study. These characteristics revealed that about 23 percent rural respondents used to earn less than USD 570 per year and about 24 percent earn less than USD 1000. As to owning the land, 25 percent of the respondents are absolutely landless and about 37 percent are marginally landless. That means about 62 percent of the rural respondents are functionally landless and or homeless. In terms of holding other assets more than 60 percent respondents possess less than USD 285. Hence, these poorest villagers usually had no other consideration than participating in MFIs.

Many respondents revealed to the interviewers that nonparticipation in MFIs mostly did not have considerations than the proverb like 'necessity knows no bound'. When they had no choice other than to borrow from the MFIs, the poor villagers became compelled to borrow from the NGOs and other MFIs. In this situation, whatever the social pressure groups suggested, it did not matter to them at all other than to go for borrowing from the MFIs. Thus, this concern might be the potential reasons for subjective norms not being statistically significant to influence the intention toward nonparticipation in MFIs.

Hypothesis 4: PBC is Positively Related with Intention toward Nonparticipation in MFIs.

Hypothesis 4 was observed not to be statistically significant. That means PBC (adjusted $R^2 = .001$, $\beta = .050$, $p > .05$, $p = 0.305$, $t = 0.1028$, F [3, 416] = 1.056) did not statistically influence the intention toward nonparticipation in MFIs. Hence, the hypothesis was not accepted.

This insignificant result can possibly be explained as follows. PBC has historically been closely related to definitive outcomes rather than future potential intention, the latter being the case for this study. Many participatory behavioral researches (Brown, 2005; Coghlan, 2005; McGehee & Norman, 2002; Thoit & Hewitt, 2001) found that past volunteer tourism experience resulted in an increase of perceived control and predicted a positive relationship between PBC and participatory intentional behavior. In contrast, this study found that PBC did not work to predict the less definitive outcome of potential intention toward nonparticipation in MFIs.

Hypothesis 5: PBC is Negatively Related with Participation or Positively with Nonparticipation in MFIs.

From the outcome of logistic regression analyses incorporating Model 1 (Table 5.5), it is observed that coefficient of PBC is -.711 with $p < .000$. The odd ratio is .491 which implies that PBC reduces nonparticipation at least by half. That means, the probability reduces or increases nonparticipation or participation by fifty-fifty. Thus, the hypothesis that postulates as PBC is negatively related with nonparticipation of the rural poor in MFIs. Hence, this hypothesis is supported by the evidence of the report.

In addition, most respondents expressed strong attitudes toward intended nonparticipation in MFIs (μ = 4.44); and Chen et al. (2001) argued that predicting behavior required specificity which was not possible given the general nature of PBC constructs. In other words, study participants could not predict with 100 percent confidence their PBC in regard to a future unpredictable event.

Hypothesis 6: Fear of Getting Into Risk of Loan is Negatively Related with Attitude toward Intended Nonparticipation in MFIs.

Hypothesis 6 was observed to be supported by the evidence. Hypothesis 6 that perceived fear of the rural poor in getting into risk of microcredit was negatively and statistically significant in relation with attitude toward intended participation (adjusted $R^2 = 0.166$, $\beta = -1.82$, $p < .01$, $t = -4.064$). The overall F [2, 417] = 42.72, ($p < .01$).

This result was consistent with many other studies (Callender & Jackson, 2005; Funk, Banldacci, Pasold & Baumgardner, 2004). Funk, et al. (2004) revealed that the effect of fear on attitude toward intention to nonparticipation was found to be statistically and negatively significant. Callender and Jackson (2005) examined the impact of fear on attitude toward intention to participate in student loans in England. The findings suggested that fear of debt affected the participation in student loan program and students from poorer backgrounds were more debt averse than those from other social classes. Specifically, the study found that debt-aversion was a significant factor for those from the lower income group, but not those from those the middle-class. Funk et al. (2004) also found similar results on the negative relationship between fear and attitude toward intended participation.

This fear was coming from social intimidation committed by the MFIs, such as confiscating cattle, roof of the houses or other valuables possessed by the rural poor (Ferdous & Uddin, 2010; Rahman, 1999). Dyal-Chand (2007) reported that the microfinance organizations used to impose human worth as loan collateral for the microfinance borrowed by the rural poor in Bangladesh. By the term human worth the author meant family status, honor and respect which, in local word, was called 'ijjat'. Examples were there that many debtors committed suicide in the extreme cases. Dyal-Chand also reported such an incident in Bangladesh where a woman captive in a house of the GB compound used her 'sari' to hang herself from the ceiling–fan having faced with the loss of honor to her family as a result to her failure to repay the loans.

As such many other social intimidations were recorded in many other studies (Kingsbury, 2007; Morduch, 1998; Rahman, 1996). Hence, fear of getting into risk of loan's negative effect on the attitude toward intended nonparticipation in MFIs was supporting the hypothesis six, which has several implications: (1) As long as this potential factor of fear of risk into microfinance borrowing has not been remove from the rural poor's mentality, the participation in MFIs will be hindered; (2) If this is the case, then the effort of alleviating rural poverty from the society will be procrastinated and development agenda of the national planning will be in jeopardy.

Hypothesis 7: Individual Preferences are Negatively Related to Attitude toward Intended Nonparticipation in MFIs.

Hypotheses 7 that individual preference of the poor villagers were observed to be negatively and statistically significant (adjusted $R^2 = 0.166$, $\beta = -3.54$, $p < .01$, $t = -7.893$). The overall F [2, 417] = 42.72, ($p < .01$).

Hence, hypothesis 7 was accepted that individual preference influences attitude toward intended nonparticipation in MFIs negatively. This evidence was consistent with other previous studies as well (Montgomery, Bhattacharya & Hulme, 1996; Mustafa, Banu, Kabir, Yusuf & Jahan, 1996; Rogaly, 1996), which indicated that nonparticipation might simply be a function of individual or household preferences that deemed that credit was not in their best short or long-term interest.

In fact, the poor villagers had very little choices in selecting by their own from which institution they would borrow the credits due to the scarcity of resources in their possession. During the survey of the present study, many nonparticipants blamed the MFIs for exploiting them in exchange of lending microcredit to the rural poor. Almost all nonparticipants in MFIs asserted that they did not have alternative options and during this sort of extreme financial crisis the poor villagers became compelled to borrow from the MFIs. If they had better economic and financial condition, they would not take any loans from MFIs (Ahmed, 2004; Rahman, 1999). Hence, this evidence appeared to be a potential reason to the rural poor's nonparticipation in MFIs.

Hypothesis 8: Religious Leaders' Lectures are Negatively Related with Subjective Norms toward Nonparticipation in MFIs.

Hypothesis 8 was not supported by the evidence to establish a significant statistical relationship, but it supported that they had a negative relationship between them. That meant religious lectures delivered by religious leaders were not statistically significant to influence subjective norms. Their relationship was observed to be negative ($\beta = -0.03$, $p > .05$, $p = .549$, $t = -.60$). This evidence was consistent with the previous studies (Ahmed, 2004; Ashraf, 2010).

Hypothesis 9: Spousal Dislike as Female Head of Household is Negatively Related with Subjective Norms toward Intended Nonparticipation in MFIs.

Among three antecedents of subjective norms, only spousal dislike as female head of household was observed to statistically significant (adjusted

R^2 = .001, β = -0.082, $p < .10$, t = - 1.616) and their relationship was found to be negative. Hence, hypothesis 9 was accepted.

This finding was consistent with Buvinic and Gupta (1997) who claimed that the socioeconomic disadvantages experienced by female-headed households, ranging from economic discrimination to social stigmatization and isolation, impeded their ability to meet the resource requirements for participation in microcredit schemes.

Hypothesis 10: Friends' Advice is Negatively Related with Subjective Norms toward Intended Nonparticipation in MFIs.

Similarly, the factor of friends' advice was also found to be statistically insignificant (β = 0.007, $p < .05$, p = 0.895, t = .132). The overall F [3, 416] = 1.197, $p > .05$, p = .31, which was also insignificant. This outcome implies that the rural poor do not care about their friends' opinion in terms of nonparticipation or participation in MFIs in Bangladesh.

Hypothesis 11: Insufficient Resources of the Rural Poor are Negatively Related with PBC toward Intended Nonparticipation in MFIs.

There are three antecedents of PBC on which hypotheses 11, 12 and 13 had been postulated. Among them, hypothesis 11 was found to be statistically significant. That is, insufficiency of resources was positively and significantly influencing the PBC (adjusted R^2 = .091, β = 0.299, $p <$ .01, t = 6.396). Hence, it was found that insufficiency of resources was statistically significant, but the sign was not supported by the evidence. Hence, the hypothesis 11 was partially supported.

Study hypothesis eleven was supported by the evidence that insufficient resources could influence PBC toward intended nonparticipation in MFIs. This influence was supported to have positive impact which was not originally postulated by the hypothesis. In this respect, hypothesis eleven was not fully supported. This finding was consistent with tourism research conducted by Phillips (2009) who examined the moderating effect of past experience over the TPB and failed to find a moderating effect of the relationship with PBC by senior citizens' casino gaming experience.

However, this result was not consistent with other studies on microfinance nonparticipation such as Evans et al. (1999), Montgomery (1996), Evans et al. (1996) and Zeller et al. (2001). Evans et al. (1999), Montgomery (1996), Evans et al. (1996) maintained that in addition to meeting eligibility criteria, MFIs required the payment of registration fees, attendance at weekly meetings and the accumulation of minimal savings.

MFIs assume, therefore, that households possess sufficient resources to meet these demands: time to attend meetings; cash reserves for savings; and energy and motivation for education and planning activities. Zeller et al. (2001) reported that available assessments of MFIs' group-based activities in Bangladesh stressed the lack of physical, human, but also social capital as the key access barriers to micro-entrepreneurship and microcredit.

Hypothesis 12: Lack of Knowledge of the Rural Poor is Negatively Related with PBC toward Intended Nonparticipation in MFIs.

Hypothesis 12 was found to be statistically significant. The factor of business knowledge possessed by the rural poor was found to be negatively and statistically significant (adjusted R^2 = .091, β = -0.083, $p < .10$, t = -1.63). Hence, the hypothesis 12 was supported by the evidence. This finding was consistent with Evans et al. (1999) which stated lack of education compromises the ability of potential clients to understand the benefits of credit. It asserted that their desire to join the program functioned within a peer group and successfully utilized credits.

Hypothesis 13: Ill-Health or Vulnerability to Crisis of the Rural Poor is Negatively Related with PBC toward Intended Nonparticipation in MFIs.

Hypothesis 13 was found to be statistically insignificant (adjusted R^2 = 0.91, β = 0.03, $p > .05$, p = 0.559, t = 0.585). That means ill-health or vulnerability to environmental crises had no statistically significantly impact on PBC. The overall F [3, 416] is 14.987 ($p < .01$). Hence, the conclusion was that hypothesis 13 was not accepted. This result is not consistent with the study such as Rahman et al. (1992) who report that participation is further constrained among potential clients suffering from ill-health or other crises that limit their capacity to acquire and utilize credit.

Table 5.11. Hypothesis and Test Results based on Logistic and Multiple Regressions

Hypothesis		Results
1	Intention is positively related with nonparticipation in MFIs	Not Supported
2	Attitudes are positively related with intention toward nonparticipation in MFIs.	Supported
3	Subjective norms are positively related with the intention toward nonparticipation in MFIs.	Not supported
4	PBC is positively related with the intention toward nonparticipation in MFIs.	Not supported
5	PBC is negatively related with nonparticipation in MFIs.	Supported
6	Fear of risk associated with loans is negatively related with attitude toward intended nonparticipation in MFIs.	Supported
7	Individual preferences are negatively related with attitude toward intended nonparticipation in MFIs	Supported
8	Religious leaders' lectures are negatively related with subjective norms toward intended nonparticipation in MFIs.	Not supported
9	Spousal dislike as female head of household is negatively related with subjective norms toward intended nonparticipation in MFIs.	Supported
10	Friends' advice is negatively related with subjective norms toward intended nonparticipation in MFIs.	Not supported
11	Insufficient resources of the rural poor are negatively related with PBC toward intended nonparticipation in MFIs.	Supported
12	Lack of Knowledge of the rural poor is negatively related with PBC toward intended nonparticipation in MFIs.	Supported
13	Ill-health or vulnerability to crisis of the rural poor is negatively related with PBC toward intended nonparticipation in MFIs.	Not supported

5.3. Chapter Summary

In the present study, we used two kinds of analytical approaches – one is the logistic regression analysis and the other is multiple regression analyses. For analyses, the study used the TPB model as the analytical framework for this study. To the best of the available knowledge of the author based on the evidence of published research, it was found that the TPB model had never been used as a predictive model of microfinance nonparticipation or participation behavior.

In this respect, it had provided the author a unique opportunity to test its predictive validity in the area of microfinance program-participation and nonparticipation by the rural poor. This study was built on previous research by identifying potential external factors that should be measured as the reasons of microfinance nonparticipation. Therefore, the extent of nonparticipation and participation had further been developed. Thus, this study had contributed to a better understanding of the wider extent of microfinance nonparticipation and participation of the rural poor in the rural areas of Bangladesh.

In the analyses, attitude was found to largely influence intention toward nonparticipation in MFIs, indicating that fear of risk associated with loans and individual preference and experience have an important impact on nonparticipation behavior of the rural poor. Thus, the relationship between intention and nonparticipation in microfinance programs are also found to be highly statistically significant which supports the validity of incorporating the TPB in the analytical framework of the study.

Subjective norms were found to be the least important predictors of microfinance nonparticipation of the rural poor where only spousal dislike as female head of household significantly influenced the intention toward nonparticipation in MFIs. However, PBC is also found to important predictors of microfinance nonparticipation directly where insufficiency of resources and lack of knowledge influenced the intention toward nonparticipation in MFIs.

It indicates that these three external factors have a vital impact on the rural poor nonparticipation in MFIs in Bangladesh. Besides, self-efficacy measures should be incorporated in microfinance nonparticipation study in order to have a better understanding of the potential reasons present in the rural society of Bangladesh.

In the logistic analyses, the study conducted the regression model with the sizes of the sample of n = 420 with both the nonparticipants and participants in MFIs. The results of regression model of n = 420 indicate that all the external variables are statistically significant except the three factors such as fear of getting into risk of loans, friends' negative advice and lack of knowledge of entrepreneurship. That means, in accordance with the opinion of both the nonparticipants and participants in MFIs, there are five potential factors that prevent the rural poor to take part in microfinance borrowing in the rural areas of Bangladesh.

This study considered only two antecedents to attitudes toward intention to microfinance nonparticipation. There may well be others that should be considered in future research, such as other aspects of attitudinal beliefs. At the same time, valid and reliable scales for these constructs needed to be developed; however, in order to include them in future studies (George, 2004).

In similar fashion, subjective norms could also consider other types referrals that were not included in the present study. So in the future, any body endeavors to attempt similar studies should address the limitations of the missing constructs of subjective norms in the domain of microfinance participation. The same suggestions are also remained with PBC which can ponder other control variables as antecedents of PBC.

The study finally intends to conclude that the theory of planned behavior proved to be a robust theoretical framework once again from which we can predict the rural poor's nonparticipation and participation in MFIs. Having a multi-dimensional approach to microfinance nonparticipation and participation along with several explanatory factors, this conceptual framework based on TPB emerged as a parsimonious construct by which it reconfirms the study of the rural poor's behavior in microfinance participation in the rural Bangladesh.

This chapter presented the results discussion and their interpretations. The study accomplished logistic analyses with dichotomous dependent variable of nonparticipation of the rural poor in MFIs. The study also incorporated the multiple regression analyses. All these analyses had been done to test altogether thirteen hypotheses. Overall, the analyses indicated that there were five variables that significantly influenced the nonparticipation variables. Thus, from the analyses it is evident that there were five variables which appeared to be responsible for impeding the rural poor's participation in MFIs in Bangladesh.

Chapter 6

CHALLENGES AND PROSPECTS

6.1. INTRODUCTION

The central focus of this study is to explore the factors that contribute to nonparticipation or participation in MFIs among the rural poor in Bangladesh which subsequently impacts on poverty alleviation and overall economic development. The study followed an exploratory approach in analyzing these issues and in looking at how the rural poor behave in terms of participating in MFIs in Bangladesh.

The primary goal of this treatise is to understand the impact of conventional interest-based MFIs on poverty alleviation along with the relevant challenges and prospects of microfinance scheme. In so doing we investigated empirically the participation patterns of the rural poor in MFIs. Once we can comprehend this pattern along with its factors that influence the participation of the rural poor in MFIs, we will be able to understand why the microfinance sector of the economy has been remained stagnant after the year 2010.

Thus, the overall goal of this study has been set to get an understanding of the factors that might have an impact on the rural poor's decision to participate or not to participate in their local MFIs in Bangladesh. To achieve this main objective, the TPB has been used as the theoretical framework for this study. The framework includes eight explanatory variables in addition to its original components of actual behavior, intention, attitude, subjective norms and PBC such as (1) fear of risk associated with loans borrowed from microfinance programs, (2) individual preferences in microfinance programs, (3) religious leaders' lecture on Islamic principles, (4) spousal dislike as female head of household (5) friends' advice, (6) insufficiency of resources, (7) lack of knowledge, and (8) ill-health or vulnerability to crisis which affect the rural poor's intention toward participation in MFIs. From the theoretical perspective, the findings of this study indicated that TPB is, in general, valid for this sample of the rural poor in the context of microfinance participation.

As the main objective of this research is to determine the hindrances to participation of the rural poor in the MFIs in Bangladesh, this study answers the following research questions within the context of current development of the microfinance sector in Bangladesh: (i) To what extent TPB explains the nonparticipation of the poor in MFIs in Bangladesh? (ii) To what extent TPB in explains intention toward nonparticipation of the rural poor in MFIs in Bangladesh? (iii) What are the factors that influence attitude of the rural poor toward MFIs in Bangladesh? (iv)What are the factors that influence subjective norm regarding MFIs among the rural poor in Bangladesh? (v) What are the factors that influence perceived behavioral control on MFIs among the rural poor in Bangladesh? In order to attain its objectives, the study applies the logistic regression technique along with the multiple regression analyses.

6.1.1. Results Based on the Overall Analyses

Study hypotheses one that intention is positively related with nonparticipation or negatively with participation in MFIs is not supported. Hypothesis two that attitude and intention toward nonparticipation in MFIs are positively related is also supported by the data. Study hypotheses three and four are not supported, but hypothesis five are supported. Hypothesis three that subjective norms and intention toward nonparticipation in MFIs are positively related is not accepted. Hypothesis four that PBC and intention toward nonparticipation in MFIs are positively related is also not supported.

Table 6.1. Summary of the logistic regression results for both nonparticipants and participants (n = 420)

Hypothesis		Results
1	Intention is positively related with nonparticipation in MFIs	Not supported
2	Attitude is positively related with intention toward nonparticipation in MFIs.	Supported
3	Subjective norms are positively related with the intention toward nonparticipation in MFIs.	Not supported
4	PBC is positively related with the intention toward nonparticipation in MFIs.	Not supported
5	PBC is negatively related with the nonparticipation in MFIs.	Supported
6	Fear of getting into risk of loan is negatively related with attitude toward intended nonparticipation in MFIs.	Supported
7	Individual preferences are negatively related with attitude toward intended nonparticipation in MFIs	Supported
8	Religious leaders' lectures are negatively related with subjective norms toward intended nonparticipation in MFIs.	Not supported
9	Spousal dislike as female head of household is negatively related with subjective norms toward intended nonparticipation in MFIs.	Supported
10	Friends' advice is negatively related with subjective norms toward intended nonparticipation in MFIs.	Not supported
11	Insufficient resources of the rural poor are negatively related with PBC toward intended nonparticipation in MFIs.	Supported
12	Lack of Knowledge of the rural poor is negatively related with PBC toward intended nonparticipation in MFIs.	Supported
13	Ill-health or vulnerability to crisis of the rural poor is negatively related with PBC toward intended nonparticipation in MFIs.	Not supported

Hypothesis five that PBC and nonparticipation in MFIs are negatively related is fully supported as well. Study hypothesis six, the negative relationship between fear of getting into risk of loans and attitudes toward nonparticipation in MFIs is fully supported. Hypothesis seven, the negative relationship between individual preference and attitudes toward nonparticipation in MFIs are fully supported as well. Hypothesis eight, the negative relationship religious leaders' lecture and subjective norms toward nonparticipation in MFIs is not supported, but the negative sign appears to be supported. Hypothesis nine, the negative relationship between spousal dislike as female head of household and subjective norms are supported fully. Hypothesis ten that negative relationship between friends' advice and subjective norms toward nonparticipation in MFIs are not supported. Study hypothesis eleven that insufficiency of resources and PBC are negatively related is supported. Hypothesis twelve, the negative relationship between lack of business knowledge and PBC are fully supported.

Finally, study hypothesis thirteen that ill-health or vulnerability to crises and PBC are negatively related was not supported at all. However, Table 6.1 summarizes the results of hypothesis testing based on logistic regression. More detailed information regarding the findings is discussed in the next section.

6.2. CHALLENGES

Based on the overall analyses, the following conclusions can be drawn about the hypotheses postulated by the present study:

This study has discussed nonparticipation and participation processes of the rural poor in MFIs and the way they are affected by different personal, psychological, socio-cultural and economic factors which control local people's livelihoods. Since independence in 1971, this South Asian nation, Bangladesh has accomplished much, but many things remain undone. Population growth becomes declined, agricultural crops output has multiplied by more than double digits, and democratic institutions are much stronger than before (Economic Census, 2013). Yet the absolute number of poor people in Bangladesh has grown steadily. Despite organized efforts to reduce poverty, almost half of the population lives below the poverty line (Ashraf, 2011c; Karim, 2011). And around 30 million people fall under the category of extreme poor (Karim, 2011).

It is evident from the past experience of entire development initiative in Bangladesh that poverty reduction has been emphasized as the highest priority. To this aim, the state agencies and other development institutions in parallel with their international donors have been seen to be active. The World Bank is the main donor and coordinator of the donor groups for aiding development process in Bangladesh (Karim, 2011). The government and the NGOs' rural development approaches were expected to work on the vision of poverty alleviation. Over the last decades the growth of NGOs and government organizations in Bangladesh has been remarkable, but major problems remain (World Bank, 2013).

Nevertheless, after playing a supervisory role in development process in Bangladesh, the World Bank has asserted in that although microcredit has proven to be an effective poverty alleviation tool it has had limited success in reaching the very poor, marginal groups who are not served by mainstream programs aimed at reaching the poor (Huq, 2001; Karim, 2011). Thus, referring GB, Rutherford (2000) advances that Muhammad Yunus, Grameen's founder and General Manager, considers that credit ought to be utilized in starting business which can set off an upward spiral of investment and income allowed the borrower to service bigger loans. That means, Dr. Yunus is more interested in 'micro-enterprise finance' (loans to start and run small business) rather than 'microfinance' (financial services for the poor) *per se*.

This development process crops up mounting debate whether microfinance programs really aid to alleviate poverty and if not, why? Research findings show that there has been participation problem arising from both sides of clients and programs of microfinance which are not effective to alleviate rural poverty (Ashraf, 2011c; Karim, 2011; Huq, 2001; Evans et al. 1999). However, the problems related to the program of microfinance are beyond the scope of this research. The prime concern of the present study is, therefore, to identify the potential problems of participation of the rural poor in MFIs in Bangladesh from the clients' point of view.

This study has focused on the rural poor who are actually surviving in the margin of society. Amidst the raging debate whether microfinance has lost its focus and turned into another tool of exploitation in the name of poverty alleviation, the rural poor women are left in a risky space. This risk is compounded by the systematic failure of many MFIs to engage the rural communities where they work in the process of designing and evaluating microfinance programs (Ferdous & Uddin, 2010). Analyzing background studies, the present treatise finds that firstly, there has been massive outreach of the poor who are deliberately excluded from the program by the MFIs. The main reason behind this is that the extreme poor are risky clients in terms of loan default.

Secondly, as with many development organizations, the voices of communities and individuals, who are the target beneficiaries of MFIs, have conspicuously lost its stream of prime target. While international donors are pressing their support in rapid implementation of MF programs in the rural areas, the impact of microfinance from the perspective of those who have the most to gain or lose from it, is crucial (Ferdous & Uddin, 2010). Because there are many incidences happened in the past in Bangladesh and elsewhere of the globe, the rural poor women are profoundly in vulnerability for which they are afraid of getting into risk of loans (Roodman, 2013). The finding of the present study is also consistent with this evidence.

Thirdly, as is mentioned earlier, there are many horror stories related to physical and sexual abuse of borrowers in the hands of the employees of MFIs. Lots of coercive measures are frequently applied when borrowers miss any of their installments. These measures include seizing the assets such as tin-roofs and walls of the houses, cattle and cooking utensils in addition to physical torturing. In this respect, the results of the present study also observe that the mental fear and intimidation (one of the external of attitude toward intended participation) in relation to the potential risk associated with microfinance significantly inhibiting the rural poor to engage in MFIs.

The study also experiences that fear of getting into risk of loans borrowed from NGO-MFIs are associated with the interest rates and other charges of microcredit which are much higher compared to market interest rates (Ferdous & Uddin, 2010). This factor also creates substantial risk or uncertainty that is compounded with suppressing the rate of returns of the business operating with funds borrowed from MFIs. Consequently, the rural poor borrowers would find it difficult to repay the loans on a weekly basis and ultimately may face a harsh tragedy. Thus, this study witnesses similarly as the findings of Ferdous & Uddin (2010) that the cause of such tragedies is being largely ascribed upon high interest rates and other charges of micro loans, which trap the borrowers into a never-ending loop.

The second external variable of this research which affects participation of the rural poor in MFIs is individual preference. In essence, it connotes individual freedom to choose whatever an individual prefers to have based on her/his capabilities. This premise of argument is echoed in Sen's thesis of "Development as Freedom" (Sen, 1999). In developing countries, one thing is missing that is entitlement which is, according to Sen, central clause to overall economic growth and development. This crucial message is absent in the microfinance programs as well. The microfinance programs are designed by the development organizations or NGO-MFIs based on their own tacit and explicit agenda which most of the times turns out contrary to the microfinance borrowers' interest. As such are group lending, weekly repaying the loan installment, weekly meeting, forced savings etc. There is no such space at all left for the individual borrowers where they can choose the loan options based on their conveniences. Thus, this factor also impasses participation in *cul de sac.*

When the rural poor speak for themselves about what they want, they ask for secured rights to land and water bodies and other agricultural, social and natural resources on which they rely to obtain a living. They want help to generate the means to improve their quality of life (Ferdous & Uddin, 2010; Huq, 2001). In this respect, Huq (2001, pp.204, 205) asserts that 'they want health care and education for their children. But economically powerful development organizations such as the Gameen Bank and BRAC, in Bangladesh, especially through their micro-credit policies, create a development world that leaves little space for local (rural poor) people to choices. The latter are obliged to accept such interventions, even when these are coercive... . Decisions about livelihoods usually generate a *disembedding* and *reembedding* of existing economic, cultural and political factors and can create new livelihood forms.' Thus, it is evident that the rural poor are not free to choose what they want to do by the borrowed funds from MFIs for their betterment of livelihoods. This factor of individual preference of the present study is so consistently found negative to significantly impact on the participation patterns of the rural poor in MFIs in Bangladesh.

The variable of religious leaders' lecture in relation to having loans from MFIs has been selected as one of the social pressures which discourage Muslims taking interest-based microloans from MFIs. Bangladesh is a Muslim majority country where 90 percent of the population is Muslims (BBS, 2013) and Islam is the state religion. Despite this fact, most of the development projects are formulated based on secular tenets of the West many of which are directly contrary to Islamic tradition and culture. So, this contrasting view of development concept creates vulnerability of local rural poor (Roodman, 2013), especially women and their empowerment. It contrasts to access to their resources in terms of networking of local people and their organizations, formulating counter-development approach and engaging people development activities such as MFIs in the pursuit of rural livelihoods. For this reason, one of the findings of the present study is that religious leaders have an influence on the lives of the people who view the activities of MFIs in negative way.

This process of religious restriction creates a conflicting space where two notions are in contrast such as conventional development interventions and local people's practices and livelihoods based on their own religious and cultural traditions which can constitute a counter-development process. Hence, the findings of this study span a wide range of socio-cultural issues in order to explore some central issues relating to the rural people's livelihoods, development initiatives and participation in these schemes. In essence, it becomes more and more difficult to ensure the rural poor participation in conventional MFIs which are frequently criticized by the religious leaders as anti-Islamic. Hence, this issue emerges as an important bottleneck of participation in the existing MFIs in Bangladesh.

The study also discovers that in contrast to these conventional, alien and stereotyped development processes guiding by foreign donors, there have been emerging many counter-development initiatives such as Islamic MFIs in Bangladesh and in many other countries of the world. Most importantly, the overall performances of these Islamic MFIs are much better than conventional MFIs in terms of many financial indicators and participation as well (Ahmed, 2012; Mannan, 2010).

The other concern of the present study is the spousal dislike as female head of household, is also related with religious and cultural contexts. As Ahmad (2009) explores his recent research in Bangladesh and finds that many husbands do not allow their wives to join NGOs for fear of backlash from religious leaders. Not only that many believe that their family integration may become vulnerable and fragile if women freely go out of home without veil for earning through borrowing funds from MFIs (Elahi & Rahman, 2006). They would freely mix up with other males who are traditionally discouraged to meet with other females. In fact, Islam does not forbid women to go out in necessity or to trade goods and services in the market, but they are instructed to do so wearing veil. Besides, Islam prioritizes male spouse as head of the family, but does not make female spouse inferior to male.

As a matter of fact, Islam puts full emphasize on a holistic view of the family which is treated as a fundamental institution of social life. So, inclusion of both spouses rather than only female spouse in borrowing loans would bring better results as is found in the case of Islamic MFIs (Ahmed, 2012). In this way, contentions between husband and wife would minimize and the family would become more integrated rather than fragile. However, the finding of this study demonstrates that this issue influences participation of the rural poor negatively. Thus, the factor of female head of household appears to be a potential hindrance to participation in MFIs in Bangladesh.

Another social referent is friend or fellow citizen who used to advice others to engage or not to engage in specific activities (Ajzen, 1991). And this factor is particularly important when the peoples are closely associated with each other in the society. In this respect, eastern tradition put much emphasizes on the advice of fellow citizens and friends or relatives. Following this fact, the present research employs friends' advice as a factor that can influence the participation of the rural poor in MFIs negatively. The result shows that though the factor is not statistically significant, its sign appears to be negative which supports partially the postulation of the study. In Bangladesh and India, there have been many undesired incidences related to the cases of default in repaying loans to MFIs. Therefore, the poor people in rural areas have become more cautious, because there is a significant risk in unqualified adoption of microcredit (Ferdous & Uddin, 2010). As is the case in Andhra Pradesh (India) that some of the loans are creating vulnerable situation to the rural poor (Roodman, 2013). Consequently, friends usually advice their fellow citizens not be involved in dealing with MFIs.

Lack of sufficient resources is another variable taken as an antecedent of PBC which can have a significant influence on nonparticipation and participation of the rural poor in MFIs that are treated as a tool of development. Rural development discourses are replete with buzzwords as such 'participation' or 'nonparticipation' is one of them. Drawing upon the reference of this participatory approach in development programs, the findings of this study is supported by Huq (2001) who mentions nonparticipation in a different light which is linked to tackling the structural causes of people's poverty, rather than putting as another input into a development project. People are poor because they are excluded and have little influence upon the forces that affect their livelihoods. Participation is part of the process whereby such people seek to have some influence and to gain access to the resources, which would help them sustain and improve their living standards. This is important in the case of Bangladesh, because majority of the poor people lack sufficient resource base for which they are considered unqualified to be a part of the development initiatives.

About 71 percent of villagers are landless in Bangladesh and it has a continuous trend (Barakat, 2013). It has been claimed by Barakat (2013) that whatever the government statistics say, the reality is that the number of poor, landless and marginal people has been increasing gradually in the country. This is, in fact, the consequence of economic growth theory that views development as a process of capital formation which, in turn, is largely determined by levels of savings and investment (Huq, 2001). As such is the Ricardian growth model, where according to this model, capital accumulation is determined not by government, but by profit-seeking capitalists. In fact, capital accumulation is the result of private investment which is funded by private savings that are verily lacked by the rural poor. For this reason, the poor have always been missing from the intervention program of the economic growth model.

Thus, Huq (2001) maintains that the intervention of microfinance, as currently practiced, is an integral wing of 'development' imposed by foreign donors such as the World Bank and does not produce 'economic growth'. Owing to this reason, after years of microfinance operations, in villages where MFIs are working, reported levels of poverty are still in the range of 50 percent to 60 percent (BBS, 2013). In this relation, it can be mentioned about the village of 'Jobra,' birthplace of microfinance which could not have attained any better living for the poor villagers than their living in the early 1970s. Thus, Hashemi and Morshed (1997, pp. 224) rightly pointed out more than a decade ago, 'the greatest obstacle that the Grameen Bank faces in providing targeted credit for poverty alleviation is poverty itself.'

Verily, the result of the present research sufficiently supports the existing reality prevailing in the contemporary rural Bangladesh where the people lack sufficient resources for which they cannot afford to take part in borrowing funds from MFIs (Evans et al. 1999). In fact, these types of the rural poor are also functionally excluded from the microfinance programs, because there are considered risky borrowers. So, they are left beyond the periphery of so-called development program. Therefore, Huq (2001) correctly ascribed this development process merely as development language or discourse. In sum, evidently insufficient resources of the rural poor are observed to be an important obstacle of participation in MFIs.

In rural Bangladesh, almost all women are deprived from having the opportunity to go to school and are thus illiterate. Just getting to be a member of the women's group, they can have a little improvement in their poor knowledge. As a matter of fact, a few poor men, also rare, have had the opportunity to receive a limited education. By and large, boys are more preferred than girls to go to school (Ferdous & Uddin, 2010; Huq, 2001).

Naturally, it appears to be an obstacle on the part of the rural poor women to participate in NGO-MFIs. Having observed this scenario in developing countries, Sen (1986) thus argues that the process of economic development through poverty alleviation must consider what people can or cannot do or be able to read and write and communicate. Illiteracy and lack of knowledge among the rural poor raise another concern. Many of the terms and conditions of MFIs are not explicit. For this reason, many women are shocked where the Grameen Bank and other NGOs deduct a percentage of their loan as savings fund which they did not know in advance.

As the case shows, this lack of knowledge and necessary education appears to be a real problem on the part of the rural borrowers in participating in MFIs. For this reason, the rural women become unable to build up their skills and equity-assets by using their active economic role. In reality, this is because of a failure to practice ‘participation’. Thus, the membership of MFIs or the participation in MFIs is the case of actually failing in preventing the rural poor’s pauperization. In this process, lack of sufficient skills and knowledge in getting funds and mobilizing these funds in the most profitable small enterprises leaves the illiterate poor women particularly vulnerable and helpless.

Ill health and vulnerability to crises was selected as another external factors linked to PBC toward intended nonparticipation in MFIs in Bangladesh. Bangladesh is a land of natural disasters with problems such as acute poverty, unemployment, meager earnings, shortage of food, malnutrition, and epidemic diseases compound vulnerability of the poor of the country exponentially, particularly the condition of rural poverty. Nevertheless, the country was able to overcome many hurdles, yet many tasks are undone. Among these undone tasks, there is illness or vulnerability to crises in rural areas especially among destitute women-folk.

One of the most important agenda of microcredit is to remove this vulnerability of the rural poor women through small credit program. Unfortunately, this important task remains until today. The results of the present study demonstrate that ill-health or vulnerability to crisis appeared to be an important impediment to ensure participation of the rural poor in MFIs. One the one hand, the destitute or extreme rural poor are excluded from the microfinance network and they fall out when they fail to pay their weekly installment due to illness or other crisis.

On the other hand, when people (borrowers) become sick and need to have medical treatment or purchase medicine, they do so in utmost secrecy to avoid field officers of MFIs. This implies that microcredit puts more emphasis on loan repayment than helping sick borrowers. Thus, Ferdous & Uddin (2010, p. 40) correctly argued that 'instead of empowering individuals and communities, repayment creates an environment of fear and intimidation where recipients must regularly sacrifice basic needs to meet an inflexible repayment schedule.'

6.3. Prospects and Recommendations

A number of findings provide suggestions for policy formulation related to microfinance programs that are primarily designed for involving the entire rural poor population in order to raise the standard of living and alleviate rural poverty which is considered as one of the most important pillars of development (Kalam, 2012). This study identified the factors faced by the rural poor for nonparticipation in MFIs. While the goals are to increase the rural poor participation in MFIs, there will be difficulties in attracting the poor people to participate actively mainly because the programs are intertwined with several potential socioeconomic bottlenecks that hinder the rural poor participation. The MFIs have to be more innovative to formulate new policy tools of operating the MFIs, so that barriers to participation in MFIs are eliminated and perceived control over certain socioeconomic parameters can be attained.

Development intervention is perceived as the execution of certain plan of actions which subsume ongoing process of social transformation embodying local people's interests and practices. The conventional development jargons view development as the implementation of Ricardian economic growth model which prioritizes capital accumulation by profit-seeking conglomerates but not by governments. This process is largely determined by the method of accumulated private savings and investments. The same approach of development is prescribed by the World Bank for the Third World communities as a whole through adopting microcredit as a generalized tool. Against this holistic view of modernization and development, like the policy planners around the globe, the prime prospects delineated by the present study are to search for other alternatives.

Finally drawing upon the findings of the present research, the study argues that microfinance authorities, development professionals and policy planners need to take full account of rural poor's livelihood practices in order to reinforce the participation of the rural poor in MFIs in Bangladesh. Only in this way, the bottlenecks that are observed in this study can be removed and the process of development can be continued through alleviating rural poverty. Otherwise, alternative measures can be adopted for attaining the new millennium goals set by Bangladesh government by the year of 2020.

References

Abraham, C. and Sheeran, P. (2003). Implications of Goal Theories for the Theories of Reasoned Action and Planned Behavior. *Current Psychology: Developmental, Learning, Personality, Social*, 22 (3): 264 – 280.

ADB (2012). News from ADB Bangladesh, *A Quarterly Newsletter*, September, 2012.

Adhikary, K. P. and Goldey, P. (2010). Social Capital and its "Downside": The Impact on Sustainability of Induced Community-Based Organizations in Nepal. *World Development*, 38(2): 184–194.

Ahmad, M. M. (2009). New Threat to Development: The Non-Governmental Organizations- Fundamentalist Conflict in Bangladesh. In F. C. Khan, A. Ahmad and M. Quddus (Eds.), *Recreating the Commons? NGOs in Bangladesh*, pp. 129 – 148, Dhaka: UPL.

Ahmed, H. (2012). Organizational Models of Islamic Microfinance. In S. N. Ali (Ed.), *Shari'a Compliant Microfinance*. pp. 17- 33, New York: Routledge.

Ahmed, S. (2009). Microfinance Institutions in Bangladesh: Achievements and Challenges. *Managerial Finance,* 35(2): 999 – 1010.

Ahmed, H. (2004). *Islamic Alternatives to Finance Poverty Focused Group-Based Microfinancing*. Paper presented at the 26th Annual Meeting of IDB with NDFIs. Tehran, September 13, 2004.

Ahmed, H. (2002). "Financing Microenterprises: An Analytical Study of Islamic Microfinance Institutions." *Islamic Economic Studies* 9(2): 27-64.

Ahmed, S. S., Narayan, A. and Zaman, H. (2009). Are the Poor Protected? Vulnerability and the Role of Safety Nets. In A. Narayan and H. Zaman (Eds.), *Breaking Down Poverty in Bangladesh*, pp. 262 – 300. Dhaka: UPL.

Ajzen, I. (2008). Consumer Attitudes and Behavior. In C. P. Haugtvedt, P. M. Herr and F. R. Cardes (Eds.) *Handbook of Consumer Psychology* (pp. 525 – 548). New York: Lawrence Earlbaum Associates.

Ajzen, I. (2007). *TPB Diagram.* <http://www.people.umass.edu/aizen/ tpb.diag.htm#null- link> accessed 28/12/2009.

Ajzen, I. (2006). *The Theory of Planned Behavior: Constructing a TPB Questionnaire.* Retrieved December 23, 2012.

Ajzen, I. (1985). From Intentions to Action: A Theory of Planned Behavior. In J. Kuhl and J. Beckman (Eds.), *Action Control: From Cognition to Behavior*, 11 – 39, Berlin,Germany: Springer.

Ajzen, I. (1987). Attitudes, Traits and Actions: Dispositional Prediction of Behavior in Personality and Social Psychology. In L. Berkowitz, *Advances in Experimental Social Psychology,* 20: 1 -61, New York: Academic Press.

Ajzen, I. (1988). *Attitudes, Personality and Behavior*. Chicago: Dorsey.

Ajzen, I. (1991). The Theory of Planned Behavior. *Organizational Behavior and Human Decision Processes,* 50: 179 – 211.

Ajzen, I. (2001). Nature and Operation of Attitudes. *Annual Review of Psychology,* Annual 2001: 27 – 57.

Ajzen, I. (2002). Perceived behavioral control, self-efficacy locus of control and the theory of planned behavior. *Journal of Applied Social Psychology,* 32: 665 – 683.

Ajzen, I. and Driver, B. L. (1992). Application of the theory of planned behavior to leisure choice. *Journal of Leisure Research,* 24, 207- 224.

Ajzen, I. and Fishbein, M. (1975). *Understanding attitudes and predicting social behaviour.* New Jersey; Prentice-Hall.

Ajzen, I. and Fishbein, M. (2000). Attitudes and the Attitude-Behavior Relation: Reasoned and Automatic Processes. *European Review of Social Psychology*, 11(1): 1 – 33.

Ajzen, I. and Fishbein (1977). Attitude-Behavioral Relations: A Theoretical Analysis and Review of Empirical Research. *Psychological Bulletin*, 84: 888 – 918.

Ajzen, I. and Fishbein, M. (1980). *Understanding Attitudes and Predicting Social Behavior.* Englewood Cliffs, N.J.: Prentice-Hall.

Ajzen, I. and Fishbein, M. (2005). The influence of attitudes on behavior. In D. Albarracin, B. T. Johnson and M. P. Zanna (eds.), *The handbook of attitudes*, Lawrence Erlbaum Associates.

Alamgir, D. A. H. (2009). *State of Microfinance in Bangladesh.* Prepared for Institute of Microfinance (InM) as part of the project on State of Microfinance in SAARC Countries.

Albarracin, D., Johnson, B. T., Fishbein, M. and Muellerleile, P. A. (2001). Theories of reasoned action and theory of planned behavior as model of condom use: A meta- analysis. *Psychological Bulletin*, 127: 142 – 161.

Ali, S. N. (2012). Introduction. In S. N. Ali (Ed.) *Sharia Compliant Microfinance,* p. 1-7. New York: Routledge.

Allen, D. (2011). *Factors influencing selected Tennessee farmers' attitudes and willingness to enter voluntary carbon market.* Unpublished PhD thesis. Tennessee State University, USA.

Alselaimi, A. (2010). *Using the Theory of Planned Behavior to Investigate the Antecedents of Physical Activity Participation among Saudi Adolescents.* Ph.D. Thesis, UUM, Malaysia.

Amin, M. R. and Sheikh, M. R. I. (2011). The Impact of Microfinance Program on the poor: A Comparative Study of Grameen Bank, BRAC and ASA in Some Selected Areas in Bangladesh. *European Journal of Business and Management,* 3(4): 346 – 364.

Amin, S., Rai, A. S. and Topa, G. (2003). Does Microcredit Reach the Poor? Evidence from Northern Bangladesh. *Journal of Development Economics*, 70(1): 59 – 82.

Anderson, D. R., Sweeney, D. J. and Williams, T. A. (2008). *Statistics for Business and Economics*. 5th Edition. Mason, OH: Thomson.

Anker, A. E., Feely, T. H. and Kim, H. (2010). Examining the Attitude-Behavior Relationship in Prosocial Donation Domains. *Journal of Applied Social Psychology,* 40(6): 1293 – 1324.

Anyanwu, C. M. (2004). *Microfinance Institutions in Nigeria: Policy, Practice and Potentials.* Paper Presented at the G24 Workshop on "Constraints to Growth in Sub Saharan Africa", Pretoria, South Africa, November 29-30, 2004.

Armendáriz, B. and Morduch, J. (2005). *The Economics of Microfinance.* Cambridge: MIT Press.

Armitage, C. J. and Christian, J. (2003). From Attitudes to Behavior: Basic and Applied Research on the Theory of Planned Behavior. *Current Psychology: Developmental, Learning, Personality, Social*, 22 (3):187 – 195.

Armitage, C. J. and Conner, M. (1999). The Theory of Planned Behavior: Assessment of Predictive Validity and Perceived Control. *The British Journal of Social Psychology*, 38: 35 – 54.

Armitage, C. J. and Conner, M. (2000). Social cognition models and health behavior: A structured review. *Psychology & Health*, 15: 173-189.

Armitage, C. J. and Conner, M. (2001). Efficacy of the Theory of Planned Behavior: A Meta- Analytic Review. *British Journal of Social Psychology,* 40: 471 – 499.

Ashraf, M. A. (2010). The Effectiveness of Microcredit Programs and Prospects of Islamic Microfinance Institutes (IMFIs) in Muslim Countries: A Case Study of Bangladesh. *Journal of Islamic Economics, Banking and Finance*, 6(4): 32 – 45.

Ashraf, M. (2011a). *Microfinance and Poverty: Mahathir's Failed Project in Malaysia: Dr Mahathir's Role in Poverty Alleviation.* Saarbrücken, Germany: Lambert Academic Publishing.

Ashraf, M. (2011b). *Microfinance or Debt Trap: Case for Yunus' Grameen Bank in Bangladesh.* Saarbrücken, Germany: Lambert Academic Publishing.

Ashraf, M. (2011c). *Demystifying Income and Nonparticipation in MFIs: Toward a Paradigm Shift.* Saarbrücken, Germany: Lambert Academic Publishing.

Ashraf, M. A. (2014). The Theory of Planned Behavior and Microfinance Participation: From the Perspective of Nonparticipating Rural Poor in Bangladesh. *Research Journal of Finance and Accounting,* 5(7): 159 – 168.

Ashraf, M. A. Alam, M. D. and Noor, M. S. I. (2010). The Influence of Privacy and Trust on the Internet Banking Adoption in Bangladesh. *Malaysian Management Journal*, 14(1& 2):13 – 23.

Ashta, A. and De Selva, R. (2012). Religious Practice and Microcredit: Literature Review and Research Directions. *Postmodern Openings,* 2(8): 33 – 44.

Avery, E. J. (2007). *Application of the theory of planned behavior to understanding voting behaviors of the young electorate.* Paper presented at the annual meeting of the International communication Association, San Francisco, CA.

Awang, Z. (2013). *Structural Equation Modeling Using AMOS Graphic.* University Technology Mara, Malaysia: Penerbit Press.

Azam, M. S. and Imai, K. S. (2009). *Vulnerability and Poverty in Bangladesh.* ASARC Working Paper, University of Manchester, UK.

Babbie, E. (2001). *The practice of social research* (9th ed.). Belmont, CA: Wadsworth/Thomson Learning.

Bamberg, S., Ajzen, I. and Schmidt, P. (2003). Choice of Travel Mode in the Theory of Planned Behavior: The Roles of Past Behavior, Habit and Reasoned Action. *Basic and Applied Social Psychology*, 25 (3): 175 – 187.

Bandura, A. (1982). Self-Efficacy Mechanism in Human Agency. *American Psychologist*, 37: 122 – 147.

Barakat, A. (2013). *Political Economy of Fundamentalism in Bangladesh.* A Report published by the Department of Economics, University of Dhaka, Bangladesh.

Bartlett, J. E., Kotrlik, J. W. and Higgins, C. C. (2001). Organizational Research: Determining Appropriate Sample Size in Survey Research.

Information Technology, Learning, and Performance Journal, 19(1): 43 – 50.

BBS (2011). Statistical Year Book 2011. *Bangladesh Bureau of Statistics* (BBS). Dhaka: BBS.

BBS (2013). Statistical Year Book 2013. *Bangladesh Bureau of Statistics* (BBS). Dhaka: BBS.

BBS (1986). Statistical Year Book 1986. *Bangladesh Bureau of Statistics* (BBS). Dhaka: BBS.

Barnes, C., Keogh, E. and Nemarundwe, N. (2001). *Microfinance Program Clients and Impact: An Assessment of Zambuko Trust, Zimbabwe. Assessing the Impact of Microenterprise Services (AIMS).* Management Systems International 600 Water Street, S.W. Washington, D.C.

Baumol, W. J., Blinder, A. S. and Scarth, W. M. (2011). *Economics: Principles and Policy,* 3rd Edition, Toronto: Harcourt.

Beadnell, B., Wilsdon, A., Wells, E. A., Morrison, D. M., Gilmore, M. R. and Hoppe, M. (2007). Intrapersonal and Interpersonal Factors Influencing Adolescents' Decision Having Sex: A Test of Sufficiency of the Theory of Planned Behavior. *Journal of Applied Social Psychology,* 37(12): 2840 – 2876.

Benkler, Y. (2006). *The Wealth of Networks: How Social Production Transforms Markets and Freedom.* New Haven, CT: Yale University Press.

Bergkvist, L. (2009). The Role of Confidence in Attitude-Intention and Belief-Attitude Relationship. *International Journal of Advertising,* 28(5): 863 – 880.

Biddle, S. J. H. and Nigg, C. R. (2000). Theories of Exercise Behavior. *International Journal of Sport Psychology,* 31: 290 – 304.

Bidin, Z. (2008). *Faktor-faktor penentu niat gelagat kepatuhan zakat pendapatan gaji* [*The factors determining the intentions of zakat obedience compliance*]. Unpublished PhD thesis, Universiti Utara Malaysia.

BIDS/IFPRI Study (1985). *Development Impact of the Food for Work Program in Bangladesh.* A Report prepared for the World Food Program, Washington, D.C.

Brann, M. and Suttan, M. L. (2009). The theory of planned behavior and college students' willingness to talk about smoking-related behaviors. *Communication Research Reports,* 26: 198 – 207.

Breivik, G. (2007). The Quest for Excitement and the Safe Society. In M. McNamee (Ed.), *Philosophy, Risk and Adventure Sports*, 10 – 24. London: Routledge

Brett, J. A. (2006). We Sacrifice and Eat Less: The Structural Complexities of Microfinance Participation. *Human Organization*, 65 (1): 8 – 19.

Broad, S. (2003). Living the Thai life – a case study of volunteer tourism at the Gibbon rehabilitation project, Thailand. *Tourism Recreational Research*, 28(3), 63-72.

Brown, S. (2005). Travelling with a Purpose: Understanding the Motives and Benefits of Volunteer vacationers. *Current Issues in Tourism* 8 (6): 479 – 496.

Brown, S. and Morrison, A. (2003). Expanding Volunteer Vacation Participation: An Exploratory Study on the Mini-mission concept. *Tourism Recreation Research,* 28: 73 – 82.

Buvinic, M. and Gupta, G. R. (1997). Female-headed households and female maintained families: are they worth targeting to reduce poverty in developing countries? *Economic Development and Cultural Change,* 45(2): 259 – 280.

Byrne, B. M. (2001). *Structural Equation Modeling with AMOS: Basic Concepts, Applications and Programming.* Mahwah, NJ: Lawrence Erlbaum Associates.

Cain, M., Khanum, S. R. and Nahar, S (1979). Class, Patriarchy and Women's Work in Bangladesh. *Population and Development Review,* 5(3): 405 – 438.

Callender, C. and Jackson, J. (2005). Does Fear of Debt Deter Students from Higher Education? *Journal of Social Policy,* 34(4): 509 – 540.

Cameron, R. (2010). *Ajzen's TPB Applied to the Use of Social Networking by College Students.* Honors Thesis, Texas State University – San Marcos.

CARE Bangladesh. (2005). *"Debt and Vulnerability in Northwest and Southeast Bangladesh: A Cross-Regional Comparison."* CARE, Bangladesh, Dhaka.

Caritas, Bangladesh (2012). *Annual Report.* Dhaka.

Casper, E. S. (2007). The Theory of Planned Behavior Applied to Continuing Education for Mental Health Professionals. *Psychiatric Services*, 58(10): 1324 – 1329.

Castells, M. (2000). *The Rise of the Network Society*. Malden, MA: Blackwell.

CDF (2017). *Annual Report 2017-18.* Credit and Development Forum, Dhaka.

CGAP, (2001). *"Linking Microfinance and Safety Net Programs to Include the Poorest: The Case of IGVGD in Bangladesh."* Consultative Group to Assist the Poor. Focus Note No. 21.

Chalmers, A. F. (2013). *What is This Thing Called Science? An Assessment of the Nature and Status of Science and Its Methods.* Hacket Publisher: Cambridge

Chatzisarantis, N. L. and Hagger, M. S. (2008). Influence of personality traits and continuation intentions on physical activity participation within the theory of planned behavior. *Psychology and Health,* 23: 347 – 367.

Chen, M. (2007). Consumer Attitudes and Purchase Intentions in Relation to Organic Foods in Taiwan: Moderating Effects of Food-Related Personality Traits. *Food Quality and Preference,* 18(7): 1008 – 1021.

Chen, I. Y. L., Chen, N. S. and Kinshuk (2009). Examining the Factors Influencing participants' Knowledge Sharing Behavior in Virtual Learning Communities. *Educational Technology and Society*, 12 (1): 134 – 148.

Christensen, R. W. and Knesek, G. A. (2009). Construct Validity for the Teachers' Attitudes toward Computers Questionnaire. *Journal of Computing in Teacher Education,* 25(4): 143 – 155.

Coakes, S. J., Steed, I. and Dzidic, P. (2006). *SPSS Version 13.0 for Windows.* Milton: John Wiley and Sons.

Cochran, W. G. (1977). *Sampling Techniques* (3rd Ed.). New York: John Wiley & Sons.

Coghlan, A. (2008). Exploring the Role of Expedition Staff in Volunteer Tourism. *International Journal of Tourism Research*, 10(2): 183 – 191.

Coghlan, A. (2005). *Toward an understanding of the volunteer tourism experience.* Unpublished PhD thesis. James Cook University, Australia.

Cohen, J., Cohen, P., West, S. G. and Aiken, L. S. (2003). *Applied multiple regression/correlation analysis for the behavioral sciences, 3rd Ed.* Mahwah, NJ: Lawrence Erlbaum Associates.

Conroy, J. and McGuire, P. (2000). *The Role of Central Banks in Microfinance in Asia and the Pacific:* Vol. 1, Overview, Manila: Asian Development Bank (ADB).

Cooper, D. R. and Schindler, P. S. (2006). *Business Research Methods.* New York: McGraw-Hill.

Copestake, J., Bhalotra, S. and Johnson, S. (2001). Assessing the Impact of Microcredit: A Zambian Case Study. *Journal of Development Studies,* 37(4): 81– 100.

Courneya, K. S. and Bobick, T. M. (2000). Integrating the Theory of Planned Behavior with the Processes and Stages of Change in the Exercise Domain. *Psychology of Sport and Exercise*, 1: 41 – 56.

CPD (2018). *Bangladesh Economy in FY 2017-18: Interim Review of Macroeconomic Performance*, Dhaka.

Daley-Harris, S. (2009*). State of the Microcredit Summit Campaign Report, 2009. A Project of RESULTS Educational Fund,* Washington, D. C. USA.

Darker, C. D. (2007). *Applying the Theory of Planned Behavior on Walking: Development and Evaluation and of Measures and an Intervention.* PhD Thesis, University of Birmingham, UK.

Delaney, J. E. (2009). *A theory of planned behavior examination of parent/adolescent drug prevention: The role that attitudes, subjective norms and perceived behavioral control play in whether parents engage in drug preventive practices.* Unpublished PhD thesis. Purdue University, USA.

Deery, M. A., Jago, L. K. and Shaw, R. N. (1998). Profiling satisfied volunteers at a tourist attraction. *The Journal of Tourism Studies*, 8(2), 18-25.

Dewhurst, M., Hancock, B. and Ellsworth, D. (2013). Redesigning Knowledge Work. *Harvard Business Review*, 90(1): 59 – 65.

Dyal-Chand, R. (2007). Human Worth as Collateral. *Rutgers Law Journal,* 38: 793 – 845.

Duong, P. B. and Izumida, Y. (2002). Rural Development Finance in Vietnam: A Macroeconomic Analysis of Household Survey. *World Development*, 30: 319 – 335.

Dusuki, A. W. (2008). Banking for the Poor: The Role of Islamic Banking in Microfinance Initiatives, *Humanomics*, 24(1): 49 – 66.

Dutta, D. and Magableh, I. (2006). A Socio-economic Study of the Borrowing Process: The Case of Microentrepreneurs in Jordan. *Applied Economics*, 38(14): 1627 – 1640.

Economic Census (2013). *Economic Census in Bangladesh. Bangladesh Bureau of Statistics*, Dhaka, Bangladesh.

Ekpe, I., Mat, N. B. and Razak, R. C. (2010). The Effect of Microfinance Factors on Women Entrepreneurs' Performance in Nigeria: A Conceptual Framework. *International Journal of Business and Social Science*, 1(2): 255 – 263.

Ekstein, K., Noack, P. and Gniewosz, B. (2013). Predictors of Intentions to Participate in Politics and Actual Behaviors in Young Adulthood. *International Journal of Behavioral Development*, 37(5): 428 – 435.

Elahi, Q. E. and Rahman, M. L. (2006). Microcredit and Microfinance: Functional and Conceptual Differences. *Development in Practice*, 16(5): 476 – 483.

Elliott, M., Armitage, C. J. and Baughan, C. J. (2007). Using the theory of planned behavior to predict observed driving behavior. *British Journal of Social Psychology*, 46: 69 – 90.

Emilus, Y. (2011). *Applying the Theory of Planned Behavior to the Problem of Employee Theft in the Retail Industry.* UMI Dissertation Publishing: ProQuest.

Evans, T. G., Adams, A. M., Mohammed, R. and Norris, A. H. (1999). Demystifying Nonparticipation in Microcredit: A Population-Based Analysis. *World Development*, 27(2): 421 – 424.

Evans, T. G., Mohammed, R., Farnsworth, J., Adams, A. M. and Chowdhury, M. (1996). *Barriers to participation in BRAC RDP.* Working Paper No. 96.01, Harvard Center for Population and Development Studies, Cambridge, MA.

Fen, Y. S. and Hong, L. K. (2009). Exercise as a Healthy Lifestyle Choice: A Review and Avenues for Future Research. *International Business Research*, 2(1): 146 - 158.

Ferdous, F. and Uddin, G. M. (2010). Microfinance. *First News*, 8 August: 36 – 47.

Fishbein, M. and Ajzen, I. (1975). *Belief, Attitude, Intentions and Behavior: An Introduction to Theory and Research.* Boston: Addison – Wesley.

Flores, N. J. (2012). *The Effect of Choice and Degree of Participation on Consumer Value and Performance Outcomes.* Unpublished PhD thesis, University of Texas Pan- America, USA.

Friedman, M. (1953). *Essays in Positive Economics.* Chicago: Chicago University Press.

Freire, P. (1970). *Pedagogy of the Oppressed.* New York: Macmillan.

Fu, F. Q., Richards, K. A., Hughes, E. D. and Jones, E. (2010). Motivating Salespeople to Sell New Products: The Relative Influence of Attitudes, Subjective Norms and Self- Efficacy. *Journal of Marketing*, 74(6): 61 – 76.

Funk, J. B., Bechtoldt-Baldacci, H., Pasold, T. and Baumgartner, J. (2004). Violence exposure in real-life, video games, television, movies, and the internet: Is there desensitization? *Journal of Adolescence*, 27: 23 – 39.

Gaeke, M. A. (2009). *Exploring Students Motivations toward Civic Engagement: An Application of Expectancy-Value Theory.* Unpublished PhD thesis, University of South California, USA.

Gagne, M. (2009). A Model of Knowledge-Sharing Motivation. *Human Resource Management*, 48(4): 571 – 589.

Galani-Moutafi, V. (2000). *The Self and the Other:* Traveler, Ethnographer, Tourist.

Gavanga, P. (2010). *Using the theory of planned behavior to predict Texas pharmacists; intention to report serious adverse drug events.* Unpublished PhD thesis. University of Texas at Austin, USA.

George, J. F. (2004). The Theory of Planned Behavior and Internet Purchasing. *Internet Research*, 14(3): 198 – 212.

GB (2011). *GB Annual Report*, Dhaka, Bangladesh.

GB (2010). *GB Annual Report*, Dhaka, Bangladesh.

Giles, M., McClenahan, C., Cairns, E. and Mallet, J. (2002). An Application of the Theory of Planned Behavior to Blood Donation: The Importance of Self-efficacy. *Health Education Research*, 19: 380 – 391.

Glass, R. D. (2001). On Paulo Freire's Philosophy of Praxis and the Foundations of Liberation Education. *Educational Researcher*, 30(2): 15 – 25.

Greenslade, J. H. and White, K. M. (2005). The Prediction of Above-Average Participation in Volunteerism: A Test of the Theory of Planned Behavior and the Volunteers Functions Inventory in Older Australian Adults. *Journal of Social Psychology*, 145(2): 155 – 172.

Guo, P. (2011). A Study on Dynamic Spatial Fixed Effect Model Based on Endogenous Initial Value. In D. W. Desheng and Y. Zhou (Eds.) *Modeling Risk Management for Resources and Environment in China*, pp. 515 – 525.

Guzarati, D. N., Porter, D. C. and Gunasaker, S. (2012). *Basic Econometrics.* New Delhi: Tata McGraw Hill.

Hair, J. F., Hult, G. T. M., Ringle, C. M., Sarstedt, M. (2013). *A Primer on Partial Least Squares Structural Equation Modeling.* Thousand Oaks: Sage.

Hair, J. F., Black, W. C., Babin, B. J., Anderson, R. E. and Tatham, R. L. (2010). *Multivariate Data Analysis* (7th ed.). Upper Saddle River, New Jersey: Pearson Prentice Hall.

Hair, J. F., Black, W. C., Babin, B. J., Anderson, R. E. and Tatham, R. L. (2009). *Multivariate Data Analysis.* New York: McMillan.

Hair, J. F., Money, A., Samuel, F. and Page, M. (2007). *Research Methods for Business.* London: John Wiley and Sons.

Hair, J. F., Black, W. C., Babin, B. J., Anderson, R. E. and Tatham, R. L. (2006). *Multivariate Data Analysis.* New York: Pearson Prentice Hall.

Hair, J. F., Black, W. C., Babin, B. J., Anderson, R. E. and Tatham, R. L. (2005). *Multivariate Data Analysis.* (6th ed.). Upper Saddle River, New Jersey: Pearson Prentice Hall.

Hartarska, V. and Nadolnyak, D. (2008). An Impact Analysis of Microfinance in Bosnia and Herzegovina. *World Development*, 26(12): 2605 – 2619.

Hasan, F. (2008). Bangladesh drowning: A reality or myth? *The Daily Star*, January 11, Dhaka.

Hashemi, S. and Rosenberg, R. (2006). *Graduating the Poorest into Microfinance: Linking Safety Nets and Financial Services*. Focus Note No. 24, CGAP.

Hashemi, S., Schuler, S. and Riley, I. (1996). Rural Credit Programs and Women's Empowerment in Bangladesh. *World Development*, 24(4): 635 – 653.

Hashemi, S. and Morshed, L. (1997). Grameen Bank: A Case Study, in Wood, G. D. and Shariff, I. A. (eds.) *Who Needs Credit? Poverty and Finance in Bangladesh.* London: Zed Books Ltd.

Hedzir, I. H. B. (2009). *Intention to Pay Zakah on Employment Income among Manufacturing Employees in Penang.* MBA Thesis, UUM, Malaysia.

Hewlett, C. L. (2008). *Political participation of nurses.* Unpublished PhD thesis, University of Maryland, USA.

Hossain, M. (1988). *Credit for Alleviation of Rural Poverty: The Grameen Bank in Bangladesh.* Research Report 65. Washington, D.C.: IFPRI/BIDS.

Hossain, M. (1985). Institutional Credit for Rural Development: An Overview of the Bangladesh Case, *Bangladesh Journal of Agricultural Economics*, 8(1): 1 – 16.

Hossain, M. (1984). *"Credit for the Rural Poor: The Experience of Grameen Bank in Bangladesh."* Research Monograph 4, Dhaka: Bangladesh Institute of Development Studies.

Huber, G. P. (2004). *The necessary Nature of Future Firms*. London: Sage.

Hulme, D. (2000). Is Microcredit Good for Poor People? A Note on the Dark Side of Microfinance. *Small Enterprise Development*, 11(1): 26 – 28.

Huq, H. (2001). *People's Practices: Exploring contestation, counter-development and rural livelihoods.* Dhaka: CDL.

Hyde, M., K. and White, K. M. (2009). Hyde, M. K., & White, K. M. (2009). To be a donor or not to be? Applying an extended theory of planned behavior to predict posthumous organ donation intentions. *Journal of Applied Social Psychology*, 39: 880-900.

IBBL (2012). *Annual Report.* Islami Bank Bangladesh Ltd. Dhaka.

Imai, K. S. and Azam, M. S. (2011). *Does Microfinance Reduce Poverty in Bangladesh? New Evidence from Household Panel Data.* Discussion Paper Series, RIEB, Kobe University, Japan.

IMF (2014). *Bangladesh: Poverty Reduction Strategy Paper.* Washington, D.C.: IMF- International Monetary Fund Publication Services.

Islam, T. (2007). *Microcredit and Poverty Alleviation.* Hampshire, England: Ashgate Publishing Limited.

Jackson, E. L. (2005). Leisure Constraints Research: Overview of a Developing Theme in Leisure Studies. In: E. L. Jackson (ed.) *Constraints to Leisure.* (pp. 3-22). State College: Venture Publishing.

Jackson, E. L. (1988). Leisure Constraints: A Survey of Past Research. *Leisure Sciences*, 10: 03 – 215.

Jackson, E. L., Quaddus, M. Islam, N. and Stanton, J. (2006). Hybrid Vigor of Behavioral Theories in the Agribusiness Research: Is it Possible? *Journal of International Farm Management*, 3(3): 1 – 15.

Jang, S. and Yoo, J. H. (2009). Topic avoidance in close relationships: Applying the theory of planned behavior. *Human Communication*, 12: 119 – 135.

Jang, S., Bai, B., Hu, C. and Wu, C. E. (2009). Affect, travel motivation, and travel intention: a senior market. *Journal of Hospitality and Tourism Research*, 33(1): 51 – 73.

Jansen, G. G. and Pippard, J. L. (1998). The Grameen Bank in Bangladesh: Helping Poor Women with Credit for Self-Employment. *Journal of Community Practice*, 5(1&2): 103 – 123.

Jefferson, U. T. (2012). *Attitudes, subjective norms and intentions regarding infant feeding methods among black college students.* PhD thesis. Saint Louis University, USA.

Jicha, K. A. (2011). *Individual-Level Predictors of Social Capital and Participation in Collective Action on the Island of Carriacou, Grenada.* Unpublished PhD Thesis, University of North Carolina State University, USA. .

Kabir, N. (2001). Conficts Over Credit: Re-Evaluating the Empowerment Potential of Loans to Women in Rural Bangladesh. *World Development*, 29(1): 63 – 84.

Kahf, M. (2004). "*Shari'ah and Historical Aspects of Zakat and Awqaf*", background paper prepared for Islamic Research and Training Institute, Islamic Development Bank.

Kaiser, F. G. and Gutscher, H. (2003). The proposition of a general version of the theory of planned behavior: predicting ecological behavior. *Journal of Applied Social Psychology*, 33(3): 586 – 603.

Kaiser, F. G. and Schultz, P. W. (2009). The Attitude-Behavior Relationship: A Test of Three Models of the Moderating Role of Behavior Difficulty. *Journal of Applied Social Psychology*, 39(1): 186 – 207.

Kalam, A. A. P. J. (2012). *Turning Points: A Journey Through Challenges.* New Delhi: Harper Collins Publishers.

Kang, H., Hahn, M., Fortin, D. R., Hyun, Y. J. and Eom, Y. (2006). Effects of perceived behavioral control on the consumer usage intentions of e-coupons. *Psychology and Marketing*, 23: 841–864.

Kaplan, D (2000). *Structural Equation Modeling: Foundations and Extensions.* Thousand Oaks, CA: SAGE.

Karim, L. (2011). *Microfinance and Its Discontents: Women in Debt in Bangladesh.* Minnesota: Minnesota University Press.

Kennedy, P. (2008). *A Guide to Econometrics.* Sixth Edition. New York: Willey- Blackwell.

Khan, A. R. (1990). Poverty in Bangladesh: A Consequence of and a Constraint on Growth. *Bangladesh Development Studies*, 18(3): 19 – 34.

Khandker, S. R. (2006). Reaching the Poor: Microfinance Experience in Bangladesh. In S. Ahmed and W. Mahmud, (eds.) *Growth and Poverty: the Development Experience of Bangladesh*, pp 237-260. Dhaka: University Press Limited.

Khandker, S. R., Koolwal, G. and Sinha, N. (2008). *Benefits of Improving Young Women's Labor Market Opportunities: Evidence from Group-Based Credit Programs in Rural Bangladesh.* World Bank Paper.

Khandker, S. R., Khalily, B. and Khan, Z. (1995*). Grameen Bank: Performance and Sustainability*, the World Bank Poverty and Social Policy Department.

Khandker, S. R. and Chowdhury, O. H. (1996). *"The Targeted Credit Programs and Rural Poverty in Bangladesh*", World Bank - Discussion Papers 337, World Bank.

Kingsbury, K. (2007), Microfinance: Lending a Hand. *The Time*, April 16, 2007.

Klein, A. and Moosbrugger, H. (2000). Maximum Likelihood Estimation of Latent Interaction Effects with the LMS Method. *Psychometrika*, 65(4): 457 – 474.

Kline, R. B. (2010). *Principles and Practice of Structural Equation Modeling* (3rd Edition). New York: Guilford Press.

Knabe, A. P. (2012). *Applying Ajzen's Theory of Planned Behavior to a Study of Online Course Adoption in Public Relations Education.* An unpublished PhD. Dissertation, Marquette University, Milwaukee, Wisconsin, USA.

Kriek, J. and Stols, G. (2010). Teachers' Beliefs and Their Interaction to Use Interactive Simulations in Their Classrooms, *South African Journal of Education*, 30: 439 – 456.

Kuotsoyannis, A. (2006). *Theory of Econometrics.* New York: Macmillan.

Lam, T. and Hsu, C. H. C. (2006). Predicting Behavioral Intention of Choosing a Travel Destination. *Tourism Management*, 27(4): 589 – 599.

Leary, K., Pillemer, J. and Wheelers, M. (2013). Negotiating with Emotion. *Harvard Business Review*, 91(1): 96 – 103.

Lee, K. (2009). *Using the Theory of Planned Behavior to Assess Participation in Congregate Meal Program.* Unpublished PhD Thesis. Kansas State University, Kansas, USA.

Lee, S. J. (2011). *Volunteer Tourists' Intended Participation: Using the Revised Theory of Planned Behavior.* PhD Thesis, Virginia Polytechnic Institute and State University, Virginia, USA.

Lee, W. H. and Moscardo, G. (2005). Understanding the impact of ecotourism resort experiences on tourists'environmental attitudes and behavioral intentions. *Journal of Sustainable Tourism*, 13(6): 546 – 564.

Lemmens, K. P. H., Abraham, C., Hoekstra, T., Ruiter, R. A. C., De Kort, W. L. A. M., Brug, J. and Schaalma, H. P. (2005). Why Don't Young People Volunteer to Give Blood? An Investigation of the Correlates of Donation Intentions Among Young Non- donors. *Transfusion*, 45(6): 945 – 955.

Li, X. (2009). *An Examination of Effects of Self-concept, Destination Personality, and SC-DP Congruence on Tourist Behavior.* Unpublished PhD Dissertation. Virginia Polytechnic Institute and State University.

Littlefield, E. and R. Rosenberg (2004). "Microfinance and the Poor: Breaking Down Walls between Microfinance and Formal Finance." *Finance Development*, June: 38 – 40.

Lockwood, N. (2011). *Motivations for Mountain Climbing: The Role of Risk.* Un- Published PhD Thesis. University of Sussex.

Mahmud, H. (2008). Unintended Consequences of Micro-Credit in Bangladesh: An Evaluation from Human Security Perspective. *Asian Social Science*, 4(10): 127 – 131.

Mahmud, S. (1994). From Women's Status to Empowerment: The Shift in the Population Policy Debate. *Bangladesh Development Studies*, 22(4): 77 – 99.

Mahmud, S. (2000). The Gender Dimensions of Program Participation: Who Joins a Microcredit Program and Why? *Bangladesh Development Studies*, 26(2&3): June- September.

Mahmud, W. (2010). Seasonal Hunger, Microfinance and Public Policy, *The Daily Star*, December 27 (Op-Ed).

Mannan, M. A. (2010). *Islamic Banking System.* Dhaka: Central Shariah Board for Islamic Banks of Bangladesh.

Manning, M. (2011). When We Do What We See: The Moderating Role of Social Motivation on the Relation Between Subjective Norms and Behaviors in the Theory of Planned Behavior. *Basic and Applied Social Psychology*, 33(4): 351 – 364.

March, R. and Woodside, A. G. (2005). Testing Theory of Planned Versus Realized Tourism Behavior. *Annals of Tourism Research*, 32(4): 905 – 924.

Mason, P. and Cheyne, J. (2000). Residents' Attitudes to Proposed Tourism Development. *Annals of Tourism Research*, 27(2): 391 – 411.

Matin, I. (undated). *Dimensions and Dynamics of MFI Competition in Bangladesh.* CGAP Note Book 1, World Bank.

McCormick, S. (2009). *Mobilizing Science: Movement, Participation and the Remaking of Knowledge.* Philadelphia, PA: Temple University Press.

McGehee, N. (2002). Alternative Tourism and Social Movements. *Annals of Tourism Research*, 29(1): 124 – 143.

McGehee, N. and Norman, W. (2002). Alternative Tourism as Impetus for Consciousness-raising. *Tourism Analysis*, 6: 239 – 251.

McGehee, N. (2002). Alternative tourism and social movements. *Annals of Tourism Research*, 29(1), 124-143.

McGehee, N. G., & Santos, C. A. (2005). Social change, discourse and volunteer tourism. *Annals of Tourism Research*, *32*(3), 760-779.

McIntosh, A. J. and Zahra, A. (2007). A Cultural Encounter through Volunteer Tourism: Toward the Ideals of Sustainable Tourism? *Journal of Sustainable Tourism*, 15(5): 541 – 556.

McTavish, D. G. and Loateher, H. J. (2002). *Social Research: An Evolving Process.* Boston: Allen and Bacon.

Menon, N. (2006). Non-Linearities in Returns to Participation in Grameen Bank Programs. *Journal of Development Studies*, 42(8): 1379 –1400.

METRIS (2009). Emerging Trends in Socio-economic Sciences and Humanities in Europe. *A METRIS* (Monitoring European Trends in Social Sciences and Humanities) Report by an Expert Group set by the European Commission, Luxemburg.

Meyer, R. L. (2002). The Demand for Flexible Microfinance Products: Lessons from Bangladesh. *Journal of International Development*, 14(3): 351 – 368.

Mitra, S. K. (2009). Exploitative Microfinance Interest Rates. *Asian Social Science*, 5(5): 87- 96.

Mohsin, A. (2005). Tourist Attitudes and Destination Marketing—The Case of Australia's Northern Territory and Malaysia. *Tourism Management*, 26: 723 – 732.

Monhartova, A. (2008). *Forming social capital: Adolescents' attitudes toward social responsibility, social activities and political participation in Czech Republic.* Tulane University, New Orleans, USA.

Montgomery, R. (1996). Disciplining or Protecting the Poor? Avoiding the Social Costs of Peer Pressure in Micro-credit Schemes, *Journal of International Development*, 8: 289 – 305.

Montgomery, R., Bhattacharya, D. and Hulme, D. (1996). Credit for the poor in Bangladesh: the BRAC Rural Development Programme and the Government Thana Resource Development and Employment Program. In D. Hulme and P. Mosley (Ed s.), *Finance against Poverty*, London: Routledge.

Moon, S. (2011). *The influence of norms music downloading intentions: Two studies.* Unpublished PhD thesis. State University of New York at Buffalo, USA.

Morduch, J. (1998). *Does Microfinance Really Help the Poor: New Evidence from Flagship Programs in Bangladesh.* Paper, Department of Economics and HIID, Harvard University, and Hoover Institution, Stanford University.

Morris, A. S. (2011). *Exploring career and technical educators' attitudes: The participation of girls' nontraditional programs of study.* Unpublished PhD thesis. University of Phoenix, USA.

Mosley, P. and Rock, J. (2004). Microfinance, Labor Markets and Poverty in Africa: A Study of Six Institutions. *Journal of International Development*, 16(3): 467 – 500.

MRA-Microfinance Regulatory Authority (2009). *An Overview of NGO-MFIs in Bangladesh.* Dhaka: MRA.

MRA (2011). *Annual Report.* Dhaka: MRA.

MRA (2010). *Annual Report.* Dhaka: MRA.

Mukherji, A. and Wright, P. (2002). Reexamining the Relationship between Action Preferences and Managerial Risk Behaviors. *Journal of Managerial Issues*, 14(3): 314 – 331.

Munday, S. and Silk, K. (2008). *Investigating discrimination in a community health department: A social norms theory and theory of planned behavior approach.* Paper presented at the annual meeting of the National Communication Association, San Diego, CA.

Mustafa S, I., Banu, A. D., Kabir, A., Mohsin, M., Yusuf, A. and Jahan, S. (1996). *'Beacon of Hope: An Impact Assessment Study of BRAC's RDP'* Research and Evaluation Division, BRAC, Dhaka

Nahas, M. V., Goldfine, B. and Collins, M. A. (2003). Determinants of Physical Activity in Adolescents and Young Adults: The Basis for High School and College Physical Education to Promote Active Lifestyles. *Physical Educator*, 60(1): 42 – 56.

Naylor, M. E. (2011). *An Alternate Conceptualization of the Theory of Planned Behavior in the Context of Sport Participation.* Unpublished PhD thesis, The Florida State University, USA.

Neal, J. D., Uysal, M. and Sirgy, M. J. (2007). The Effect of Tourism Services on Travelers' Quality of Life. *Journal of Travel Research*, 46:154-163.

Neidhart, M. W. (2005). *Participation: A model of individual willingness to participate in the transportation planning process.* Unpublished PhD thesis. University of Central Florida, USA.

New Age (March 17, 2018). *Bangladesh meets all criteria to be a developing country*. Page 8.

NFPCSP (2007). "*A Research Needs Digest for Food Security in Bangladesh*", Technical Report # 2, Dhaka: Bangladesh.

Noble, C. A. (2010). *Small Plots, Big Hopes: Factors Associated with Participation in Garden Project in Lesotho*. Unpublished MA Thesis. University of South Florida, Florida, USA.

Notani, A. S. (1998). Moderators of Perceived Behavioral Control' Predictiveness in the Theory of Planned Behavior: A Meta-Analysis. *Journal of Consumer Psychology*, 7(3): 247 – 271.

Nunnally, J. C. (1978). *Psychometric Theory.* New York: McGraw-Hill.

Oh, H. and Hsu, C. H. C. (2001). Volitional degrees of gambling behavior. *Annals of Tourism Research*, 28(3): 618 – 637.

Okun, M. A. and Sloane, E. S. (2002). Application of Planned Behavior Theory to Predicting Volunteer Enrollment by College Students in a Campus-Based Program. *Social Behavior and Personality*, 30(3): 243 – 250.

Omoro, N. O. (2013). The Utilization of Microfinance Loans and Household Welfare in the Emerging Markets. *European International Journal of Science and Technology*, 2(3): 59 – 78.

Pallant, J. (2011). *SPSS Survival Manual: A Step by Step Guide to Data Analysis Using SPSS for Windows*. Crows Nest: Allen and Unwin.

Pallant, J. (2007). *SPSS Survival Manual: A Step by Step Guide to Data Analysis Using SPSS for Windows.* (2nd Ed.). Crows Nest: Allen and Unwin.

Park, H. S. and Lee, D. W. (2009). A Test of Theory of Planned Behavior in Korea: Participation in Alcohol-Related Social Gatherings. *International Journal of Psychology*, 44(6): 418 – 433.

Park, A and Ren, C. (2001). Microfinance with Chinese Characteristics. *World Development*, 29: 39 – 62.

Payton, K. G. (2011). *Effects of attitudes, subjective norms, self-efficacy and Bike Rodeo participation on intention to Bike safely.* Unpublished PhD thesis. Arizona State University, USA.

Phetvaroon, K. (2006). *Application of the Theory of Planned Behavior to Select a Destination after a Crisis: A Case Study of Phuket, Thailand.* Unpublished PhD dissertation. Oklahoma State University.

Phillips, W. J. (2009). *Senior Casino Motivation and Gaming Intention: An Extended Theory of Planned Behavior Model.* Unpublished PhD Thesis. Kansas State University, Kansas.

Pine, D. (2010). *The Microfinance Sector in Bangladesh: Innovation or Stagnation.* BA Thesis in Banking and Fnance, Zurich: University of Zurich.

Povey, R., Conner, M., Sparks, P., James, R. and Shepherd, R. (2000). Application of the Theory of Planned Behavior to Two Dietary Behaviors: Roles of Perceived Control and Self-efficacy. *British Journal of Health Psychology*, 5(2): 121 – 139.

Powell, W. and Snellman, K. (2004). The Knowledge Economy. *Annual Review of Sociology*, 30: 199 – 221.

PPRC (2006). *Governance Survey.* Power and Participation Research Center, Dhaka.

PKSF (2009). *PKSF, "PKSF Profile",* Website of the PKSF, accessed on 09/02/2009 http://www.pksf-bd.org/about_pksf.html.

Rahman, A. (2001*). Women and Microcredit in Rural Bangladesh: An Anthropological Study of Grameen Bank Lending.* Colorado: Westview Press.

Rahman, A. (1999). Microcredit Initiatives for Equitable and Sustainable Development: Who Pays? *World Development*, 27(1): 67 – 82.

Rahman, A. (1996), "Microcredit for Women in Rural Bangladesh: Retrenchment of Patriarchal Hegemony as a Consequence", *Chicago Anthropology Exchange*, 23: 6 – 22.

Rahman, H. S., Hossain, M., Chowdhury, O. H., Sen, B. and Hamid, S. (1992). *Rethinking Rural Poverty: The Case of Bangladesh,* Bangladesh Institute of Development Studies, Dhaka, Bangladesh.

Rahman, H. Z. (2009). Poor and Governance Process in Bangladesh. In A. Narayan and H. Zaman (Eds.), *Breaking Down Poverty in Bangladesh*, pp. 301 – 321. Dhaka: UPL.

Rahman, M. F. (2010). Microlenders Get Uniform Rate. *Daily Star* (Newspaper), November 9, Dhaka.

Rahman, S. M. (2000). Microfinance Status in Bangladesh and Forthcoming Challenges. *Holiday,* June 15.

Rashid, L. (2010). Microfinance Regulation in Bangladesh: Development and Experiences. *A Paper presented in the International Conference on "Microfinance Regulation: Who Benefits?" arranged by the Micro Credit Regulatory Authority (MRA) of Bangladesh,* 15 – 17 March, Dhaka.

Razzaque, M. A. (2010). Microfinance and Poverty Reduction: Evidence from a Longitudinal Household Panel Database. *The Bangladesh Development Studies*, 33(3): 47 – 68.

Raymond, E. M. and Hall, C. M. (2008). The development of cross-cultural (mis)understanding through volunteer tourism. *Journal of Sustainable Tourism.* 16(5): 530 – 543.

Rice, J. (2011). *Examining black and white men's willingness to participate in domestic violence prevention activities.* Unpublished PhD thesis. Morgan State University, USA.

Rivis, A. and Sheeran, P. (2003). Descriptive Norms as an Additional Predictor in the Theory of Planned Behavior: A Meta-Analysis. *Current Psychology: Developmental, Learning, Personality, Social,* 22(3): 218 – 233.

Robles-Fernandez, R. (2011). *Youth engagement: A study of the impacts of students' beliefs and attitudes toward civic participation.* Unpublished PhD thesis. City University of New York, USA.

Rogaly, B. (1996). Micro-finance evangelism,'destitute women', and the hard selling of a new anti-poverty formula", *Development in Practice,* 6(2): 100 – 112.

Roodman, D. (2013). *The State of Microcredit. A Report published by the Center for Global Development.* http://www.cgdev.org/blog/state-microcredit. Retrieved on April 24, 2014.

Rubin, A. and Babbie, E. (2005). *Research Methods for Social Work.* Belmont, CA: Brooks.

Rutherford, S. (2003). "Raising the Curtain on the 'microfinancial service era'", in Harper, M. (ed.) *Microfinance: Evolution, Achievements and Challenges*, London: ITDG Publishing.

Sachs, J. D. (2005). *The End of Poverty. Economic Possibilities for our Time.* New York: Penguin. p. 20.

Schiffman, L. G. and Kanuk, L. L. (2000). *Consumer Behavior.* 7th edition, Upper Saddle River, NJ: Prentice-Hall.

Schumacker, R. E. and Lomax, R. G. (2011). *A Beginner's Guide to Structural Equation Modeling* (3rd ed.). Mahwah, N. J.: Lawrence Erlbaum Associates.

Schwiecker, S. (2004). *The Impact and Outreach of Microfinance Institutions: The Effect of Interest Rates.* Unpublished Master's Thesis in the University of Tübingen, Germany.

Sen, A. K. (1982). The Food Problem: Theory and Policy. *Third World Quarterly*, 4: 447 – 459.

Sen, A. K. (1999). *Development as Freedom.* New York: Oxford University Press.

Sen, B. and Hulme, D. (2006). *"The State of the Poorest in Bangladesh: Tales of Ascent, Descent, Marginality and Persistence."* A Joint Study of Bangladesh Institute of Development Studies (BIDS) and Chronic Poverty Research Centre (CPRC) of UK.

Sengupta, R. and Aubuchon, C. P. (2008). The Microfinance Revolution: An Overview. *Federal Reserve Bank of St. Louis Review*, 90(1): 9 – 30.

Shukran, M. K and Rahman, F. (2011). *A Grameen Bank Concept: Micro-Credit and Poverty Alleviation Program in Bangladesh.* Paper presented to International Conference on Emerging Trends in Computer and Image Processing (ICETCIP'2011), Bangkok, December.

Siegel, J. T., Alvaro, E. M., Lac, A. Crano, W. D. and Dominick, A. (2008). Intentions of becoming a living organ donor among Hispanics. A theory-based approach exploring differences between living and nonliving organ donation. *Journal of Health Communication*, 13(1): 80 – 99.

Sinclair, M. (2007). Editorial: A guide to understanding theoretical and conceptual frameworks. *Evidence Based Midwifery*, 5(2): 39.

Smith, J. R., Terry, D. J., Manstead, A. S. R., Louis, W. R. Kotteman, D. and Wolfs, J. (2008). The Attitude-Behavior Relationship in Consumer Conduct: The Role of Norms, Past Behavior and Self-Identity. *Journal of Social Psychology*, 148(3): 311 – 334.

Sommer, L. (2011). The Theory of Planned Behavior and the Impact of Past Behavior. *International Business and Economics Research Journal*, 10(1): 91 – 110.

Stedman, R. (2002). Toward a Social Psychology of Place: Predicting Behavior from Place- Based Cognitions, Attitude and Identity. *Environment and Behavior*, 34(5): 561 – 581.

Stoddart, H. and Rogerson, C. M. (2004). Volunteer Tourism: The Case of Habitat for Humanity in South Africa. *GeoJournal*, 60(3): 311 – 318.

Stout, J. (2012). *Pediatric dentists' willingness to participate in practice based research networks.* Unpublished PhD thesis. University of Washington, USA.

Sue, C. (2009). *An exploratory mixed methods study of Taiwanese junior college learners' attitudes toward their participation in Literature Circles.* Texas A & M University, USA.

Suhayati, E. (2012). The Influence of Audit Fee, Audit Time Budget Pressure and Public Accountant Attitude on the Public Accounting Dysfunctional Behavior and Its Implication on Audit Quality Survey on "Small" Scale Public Accounting Firms in Java. *Journal of Global Management*, 4(1): 1 – 24.

Sun, X., Guo, Y., Wang, S. and Sun, J. (2006). Predicting Iron-fortified Soy Sauce Consumption Intention: Application of the Theory of Planned Behavior and Health Belief Model. *Journal of Nutrition Education and Behavior*, 38(5): 276 – 285.

Swain, R. B. and Floro, M. (2008). *Effect of Microfinance on Vulnerability, Poverty and Risk in Low Income Households*. Working Paper, Department of Economics, American University, Washington, D.C., USA.

Symons, D. and Hausenblas, H. A. (2003). Exercising for Two: Examining Pregnant Women's Second Trimester Exercise Intention and Behavior Using the Framework of the Theory of Planned Behavior. *Women's Health Issues*, 13: 222 – 228.

Tarraf, W. F. (2010). *The role of religion in structuring their civic and political attitudes and behavior,* Unpublished PhD thesis. Wayne State University, Detroit, Michigan, USA.

Teece, D. (2003). Expert Talent and the Design of (professional service) Firms. *Industrial and Corporate Change*, 12(4): 895 – 916.

Thoits and Hewitt (2001). Volunteer work and well-being. *Journal of Health and Social Behavior*, 42: 115 – 131.

Townsend, R. M. (2003). Micro Credit and Mechanism Design. *Journal of the European Economic Association*, 1(2): 468 – 477.

The Economist (2000). *The Other Government in Bangladesh,* Opinion, 30(12).

Ting, J. Y. C. (2010). *Understanding Asian American and Latino Symptom-specific Help- seeking attitudes.* Unpublished PhD thesis. University of Utah, USA.

Ullah, A. K. M. A. and Routray, J. K. (2007). Rural poverty alleviation through NGO interventions in Bangladesh: how far is the achievement? *International Journal of Social Economics,* 34(4), 237 – 248.

UNDP (2014). *Human Development Report.* New York: UNDP

van den Hooff, B. and de Ridder, J. A. (2004). Knowledge Sharing in Context: The Influence of Organizational Commitment, Communication Climate, and CMC Use on Knowledge Sharing. *Journal of Knowledge Management*, 8(6): 117 – 130.

Venkatesh, V. and Davis, F. D. (2000). A Theoretical Extension of the Technology Acceptance Model: Four Longitudinal Field Studies. *Management Science,* 9.

von Linden, M. (2010). *The theory of planned behavior as a predictor of sleep hygiene and sleep quality.* Unpublished PhD thesis. Saint Louis University, USA.

Wahid, A. N. M. (1999). The Grameen Bank and Women in Bangladesh. *Challenge*, 42(5): 94 - 101.

Wahid, A. N. M. (1996). *The Grameen Bank: Poverty Relief in Bangladesh.* San Francisco: Westview Press.

Walker, S. and Matin, I. (2006). Changes in the Lives of the Ultra-Poor. *Development in Practice*, 16(1): 80 – 84.

Wang, X. (2009). Integrating the theory of planned behavior and attitude functions: Implications for health campaign design. *Health Communication*, 24: 426 – 434.

Wattanakamolchai, S. (2008). *The Evaluation of Service Quality by Socially Responsible Customers.* Unpublished PhD Thesis. Virginia Polytechnic Institute and State University, Virginia.

Wearing, S. (2001). *Volunteer tourism experiences that make a difference.* Oxon, CABI.

Weijeters, B., Cabooter, E. and Schillewaert, N. (2010). The effect of rating scale format on response styles: The number of response categories and response category labels. *International Journal of Research in Marketing, 27*, 236-247.

Weiss, J. and Montgomery, H. (2005). Great Expectations: Microfinance and Poverty Reduction in Asia and Latin America. *Oxford Development Studies,* 33(3&4): 391 – 416.

White, K. M. and Wellington, L. (2009). Predicting Participation in Group Parenting Education in an Australian Sample: The Role of Attitudes, Norms and Control Factors. *Journal of Primary Prevention*, 30(2): 173 – 189.

Woller, G. (2002). From Market Failure to Marketing Failure: Market Orientation as the Key to Deep Outreach in Microfinance. *Journal of International Development*, 14: 305 – 324.

Wood, M. E. (2008). Theoretical Framework to Study Exercise Motivation for Breast Cancer Risk Reduction. *Oncology Nursing Forum*, 35 (1): 89 – 96.

World Bank (2013). *World Bank Indicators Database,* Washington, D.C.: The World Bank.

World Bank (2014). *World Bank Indicators Database,* Washington, D.C.: The World Bank.

Wuestewald, T. (2012). *The structural relationships among employee participation, socio-moral climate, engagement, and civic attitudes in a political context.* Unpublished PhD thesis. Oklahoma State University, USA.

Yunus, M. (1997). The Grameen Bank Story: Rural Credit in Bangladesh. In A. Krishna, N. Uphoff and M. J. Esman (eds.) *Reasons For Hope: Instructive Experiences in Rural Development,* pp. 9-24. Kumarian Press, London.

Yunus, M. (1976). *Betoil Gramer Jarimon, Karimon abong Anayannora,* Dhaka: University Press Limited (A Book in Bengali Language).

Yusoff, A., Rahman, A. S. and Shapiin, M. N. (2006). A Study on the Possibility of Mosque Institution Running a Micro-Credit Program Based on the Grameen Bank Group Lending Model: The Case of Mosque Institution in Kelantan, Malaysia. *Mosques for Micro-Credit Program*, 189 – 204.

Zaman, H. (2004). "*The Scaling-up of Microfinance in Bangladesh: Determinants, Impact and Lessons.*" World Bank Policy Research Working Paper Series, No. 3398.

Zeller, M. S., Ahmed, M. and Rashid, A. U. S. (2001). *Group-Based Financial Institutions for the Rural Poor in Bangladesh.* Research Report No. 120. IFPRI, Washington, D.C., USA.

Zikmund, W. G. (2005). *Business Research Methods*. Ohio: Thomson.

Zhou, L. (2007). Application of TPB to punctuation usage in instant messaging. *Behavior and Information Technology,* 26: 399 – 407.

Zini, D. M. (2002). *Participation Decisions by Labor Union Members: The Theory of Planned Behavior and Personality*. PhD Thesis, McMaster University.

Zohir, S. (2001). *Understanding the Nature of MFI participation: Evidence from Bangladesh, in Monitoring and Evaluations of Microfinance Institutions.* Final Report, Bangladesh Institute of Development Studies, Dhaka.

APPENDIX: SURVEY OF PARTICIPATION (NONPARTICIPATION) IN MFIS

Section A

Please answer all questions by circling the number that best represents your opinion as objectively and honestly as you possibly can.

1. Do you know about the existence of MFIs (institutions giving loans to the poor)?	❑ Yes	❑ No If "No", please go straight to **Section F**
2. Are you participating in MFIs now?	❑ Yes	❑ No

Section B

Please answer all questions by circling the number that best represents your opinion as objectively and honestly as you possibly can.

	Strongly disagree	Disagree	Either disagree nor agree	Agree	Strongly agree
Intention					
1. I am eager to participate in the MFIs.	1	2	3	4	5
2. I plan not to participate in the MFIs in the future.	1	2	3	4	5
3. I intend to participate in the MFIs in the future.	1	2	3	4	5
4. I don't expect to participate in the MFIs in the future.	1	2	3	4	5
5. I intend to participate in Islamic MFIs.					
Attitude					
1. I believe that participation in MFIs is a good idea.	1	2	3	4	5
2. I believe that participation in MFIs is a bad idea.	1	2	3	4	5
3. I believe that participation in Islamic MFIs is a bad idea.	1	2	3	4	5
4. I believe that participation in Islamic MFIs is a good idea.	1	2	3	4	5
5. I believe that I should participate in MFIs.	1	2	3	4	5
6. I believe that I should not participate in MFIs.	1	2	3	4	5
7. I consider that the MFIs are good to increase income.	1	2	3	4	5
8. I feel that the MFIs are charging a high interest rate.	1	2	3	4	5
9. I feel that the risks are high in participating in MFIs.	1	2	3	4	5
10. I feel that the MFIs are against the religion of Islam.	1	2	3	4	5
11. I feel that women should not be involved in MFIs by violating *purdah.*	1	2	3	4	5
12. I believe that I should not be involved in interest-based MFIs.	1	2	3	4	5
Subjective Norms					
1. My religious leaders inspire me to participate in MFIs.	1	2	3	4	5
2. My spouse encourages my participation in MFIs.	1	2	3	4	5
3. My friends advise me to participate in MFIs.	1	2	3	4	5
Perceived Behavioral Control					
1. I am constrained by insufficient resources.	1	2	3	4	5
2. I am constrained by lack of proper knowledge of business.	1	2	3	4	5
3. I am constrained by poor health or I am vulnerable to crises.	1	2	3	4	5

Section C (Antecedents of Attitude)

Please answer all questions by circling the number that best represents your opinion as objectively and honestly as you possibly can.

	Strongly disagree	Disagree	Either disagree nor agree	Agree	Strongly agree
Fear of Risk Associated with Loans					
1. I believe that I will be in financial trouble taking loans from MFIs.	1	2	3	4	5
2. I believe that I will not be able to repay the loans on a weekly basis.	1	2	3	4	5
3. I believe that I will be losing my other belongings if I become a default.	1	2	3	4	5
4. I believe that I will not get out of the loans once I take it from MFIs.	1	2	3	4	5
Individual Preference					
1. I believe that I should not take loans from MFIs.	1	2	3	4	5
2. I believe that I should take loans from commercial banks.	1	2	3	4	5
3. I believe that I should take loans from NGOs.	1	2	3	4	5
4. I believe that I should take loans from village money lenders.	1	2	3	4	5
5. I believe that I should take loans from friends or relatives.	1	2	3	4	5

Section D (Antecedents of Subjective Norms)

Please answer all questions by circling the number that best represents your opinion as objectively and honestly as you possibly can.

	Strongly disagree	Disagree	Either disagree nor agree	Agree	Strongly agree
Religious Advice					
1. My religious leaders believe that I should not take loans from MFIs because it is based on interest which is forbidden in religion.	1	2	3	4	5
2. My religious leaders believe that that MFIs are spreading anti-Islamic system in society.	1	2	3	4	5

	Strongly disagree	Disagree	Either disagree nor agree	Agree	Strongly agree
3. My religious leaders believe that I would be in risk of taking loans from MFIs.	1	2	3	4	5
4. My religious leaders believe that I may face social isolation in participating in MFIs.	1	2	3	4	5
Female Head of Household					
1. My spouse believes that female head of household is undesirable.	1	2	3	4	5
2. My spouse believes that female should remain in the house to comply with *purdah.*	1	2	3	4	5
3. My spouse believes that female should not be involved in business outside home.	1	2	3	4	5
Friend's Advice					
1. My friends believe that I should be abstain from taking loans form MFIs.	1	2	3	4	5
2. My friends believe that I should take loans from commercial banks.	1	2	3	4	5
3. My friends believe that I should take loans from relatives or friends.	1	2	3	4	5
4. My friends believe that I would be in risk of taking loans from MFIs.	1	2	3	4	5

Section E (Antecedents of Perceived Behavioral Control)

Please answer all questions by circling the number that best represents your opinion as objectively and honestly as you possibly can.

	Strongly disagree	Disagree	Either disagree nor agree	Agree	Strongly agree
Insufficient Resources					
1. I believe that I have financial ability to pay registration fees for taking loans	1	2	3	4	5
2. I believe that I have time to attend weekly meetings	1	2	3	4	5
3. I know that I have cash money for savings.					
4. I believe that I have energy and motivation for MF activities	1	2	3	4	5
Lack of Business Knowledge					
1. I believe that I have sufficient business knowledge to invest loan money in successful enterprises.	1	2	3	4	5

	Strongly disagree	Disagree	Either disagree nor agree	Agree	Strongly agree
2. I believe that I have sufficient financial knowledge to mobilize loan money.	1	2	3	4	5
3. I believe that I have sufficient marketing knowledge to sell the products of my micro-enterprise.	1	2	3	4	5
4. I believe that I have other skills of doing business.	1	2	3	4	5
Poor Health or Vulnerability to Crises					
1. I feel that my physical health condition is sound to utilize loans.	1	2	3	4	5
2. I feel that my mental health is sound to operate loans.	1	2	3	4	5
3. I believe that environmental disaster may hamper operating loans.	1	2	3	4	5

Section F

Please answer all questions by ticking ☑ the box that best represents yourself.

Sex:	❑ Male	❑ Female		
Age:	❑ 15 – 25	❑ 26 – 40	❑ 41 – 55	❑ 56 – 60
Marital status:	❑ Single	❑ Married	❑ Divorced	
Education:	❑ Primary school ❑ Diploma	❑ High school ❑ Degree/Bachelor	❑ College/Certificate	
Yearly household income:	❑ 0 – 20000 ❑ 700001 – 100000	❑ 20001 – 40000 ❑ More than 100000	❑ 400001 – 70000	
Total amount of land (including home land) (in decimal):	❑ 0 ❑ More than 100 decimal	❑ 1 – 33	❑ 34 – 66 ❑ 67 – 100	
Other assets (in Taka):	❑ 0 – 20000 ❑ 700001 – 100000	❑ 20001 – 40000 ❑ More than 100000	❑ 400001 – 70000	

Thank you very much for your time

ABOUT THE AUTHOR

Mohammad Ali Ashraf, PhD

Department of Economics, United International University,
United City, Bangladesh

Education: BSc Agricultural Economics (BAU-Bangladesh Agricultural University), MA Economics (uOttawa-University of Ottawa, Canada), PhD in Financial Economics (UUM- Northern University of Malaysia)

Research and Professional Experience: Five Years' Corporate Job Experience, Five Years' Research Experience and Sixteen Years' Teaching Experience.

Professional Appointments: Consultancy in many national and international NGO-MFIs.

Publications from the Last 3 Years:

Ashraf, M.A. (2019). *Gender Impact and Mediating Influence of Job Satisfaction between Compensation and Commitment of the Faculty Members in Private Universities in Developing Context: An Analysis Using SEM. Management: Journal of Contemporary Management Issues* (In Review) Scopus indexed and Thompson Reuters

Ashraf, M.A. (2019). Theory of Boundedly Rational Planned Behavior: A New Model, *Zagreb International Review of Economics and Business*. (In Review) Scopus and Thompson Reuters

Ashraf, M. A. (2018). *Use of Bounded Rationality Theory to Understand Participation of Rural Women in Islamic Microfinance: An Analysis Using SEM. Entrepreneurship, Microfinance and Development, 29(1): 1 – 23.* http://dx.doi.org/10.3362/1755-1986.18-00005, Scopus indexed.

Ashraf, M.A. (2019). Theory of Islamic Entrepreneurship: A Conceptual Paper, *Social Enterprise Journal* (In Review) Scopus Indexed

Ashraf, M. A. (2018). Consumers' Anti-Consumption Behavior toward Organic Food Purchase: An Analysis Using SEM. *British Food Journal (Forthcoming), Emerald Journal*, Scopus Indexed

Ashraf, M.A. (2018). Mediation of Faculty Retention between Specific HRM Practices and Quality Higher Education in Developing Context: An Analysis Using SEM. *Journal of Education*, (In Review)

Ashraf, M.A. (2018). Mediation of Faculty Retention between Specific HRM Practices and Quality Higher Education in Developing Context: An Analysis Using SEM. *Journal of Education*, (In Review) Scopus Indexed.

Ashraf, M. A. (2019). Influences of Working Condition and Faculty Retention on Quality Education in Private Universities in Bangladesh: An Analysis Using SEM. *International Journal of Educational Management*, 33(1): 1 – 20. *Emerald Journal*, Scopus Indexed.

Osman, AZMR, Ashraf, M. A. (2017). The Nordic Model and Service Quality Education from the Perspectives of International Students: Evidence from Malaysia. *Iranian Journal of Management Studies (forthcoming),* Scopus/Thompson Reuters.

Ashraf, M.A., Osman, A.Z.R and Ratan, S.R.A. (2016). Determinants of Quality Education in Private Universities from the Students' Perspectives: A Case Study in Bangladesh, Quality Assurance in Education, 24(1): 123 – 138. Scopus/Thompson Reuters (Emerald Pub)

Ashraf, M. A. (2018). *HRM Practices and Quality Education in Private Universities: An Empirical Study in Bangladesh*. (In Progress)

Ashraf, M. A. (2018). *Mediating Influences of Compensation Structure and Job Satisfaction between Gender Difference and Organizational Commitment.* (In progress)

Ashraf, M. A. (2018). The Mediating Role of Work Atmosphere in the Relationship between Supervisor Cooperation, Career Growth and Job Satisfaction. *Journal of Workplace Learning, (Forthcoming) Scopus Indexed Emerald Journal*

Ashraf, M. A. (2017). Effects of Faculty Supervisor Support and Job Autonomy on Quality Education Mediated by Working Condition: An Investigation Using SEM. *Higher Education Quarterly*, (In Review) (Scopus Indexed Journal)

Ashraf, M.A. (2018). Consumer Behavior in Halal Food Purchase in Bangladesh: An Analysis Using SEM, *Journal of Islamic Marketing (Forthcoming)*, Emerald and Scopus Indexed.

Ashraf, M. A. (2019). Quality Management and Specific HRM Practices in Tertiary Education: Does Faculty Commitment Mediate? *International Review of Education (In Review)* Scopus Indexed.

INDEX

A

B

C

D

E

F

G

H

I

K

L

M

N

O

P

R

S

Poverty: Global Perspectives, Challenges and Issues of the 21st Century

Editor: Cecilia Schultz

Series: Hunger and Poverty: Causes, Impacts and

Book Description: Poverty in modern societies has been of utmost importance and always is considered as a global issue. Most economic policies of governments have direct impacts on reducing or increasing the number of poor people in the society. However, a significant number of people in developing countries still live in poverty. This book reviews global perspectives, challenges and issues of the 21st century that poverty poses.

Hardcover ISBN: 978-1-53610-250-5
Retail Price: $95

Poverty: Global Challenges, Role of Inequality and Reduction Strategies

Editor: Chukwuma Agu

Series: Hunger and Poverty: Causes, Impacts and Eradication

Book Description: This book shows why poverty may not have been responsive to growth in developing countries in recent years. It examines outcomes of policies and insists that poverty, inequality and reduction strategies need not only be context-specific, but should involve much more than just narrow interventions.

Hardcover ISBN: 978-1-63482-304-3
Retail Price: $230

Measures of Poverty: Selected Reports from the U.S. Census Bureau

Editor: Isaac Henson

Series: Hunger and Poverty: Causes, Impacts and Eradication

Book Description: This book describes individuals and families living near poverty- those individuals whose family incomes are close to, but not below, official poverty thresholds. It also presents data on poverty based on information collected in the Survey of Income and Program Participation (SIPP); and describes patterns of poverty using measures with different time horizons and provides a dynamic view of the duration of poverty spells and the frequency of transitions into and out of poverty.

eBook ISBN: 978-1-63463-271-3
Retail Price: $120

The War Against Poverty: Progress and Status, Fifty Years On

Editor: Adnan Keoni

Series: Hunger and Poverty: Causes, Impacts and Eradication

Book Description: This book provides a progress report of poverty 50 years later as well as insight on the poverty levels of the United States in 2012.

Hardcover ISBN: 978-1-63117-421-6
Retail Price: $130